Political Voice

Institute for Social Science Research

Monograph Series

General Editor: Philip B. Coulter

Political Voice: Citizen Demand for Urban Public Services, by Philip B. Coulter

Political Voice

Citizen Demand for Urban Public Services

Philip B. Coulter

With a Foreword by
Richard Arrington, Jr.

Published for the
Institute for Social Science Research by
The University of Alabama Press   *Tuscaloosa and London*

Copyright © 1988 by
The University of Alabama Press
Tuscaloosa, Alabama 35487
All rights reserved
Manufactured in the United States of America

Second Printing 1991

Library of Congress Cataloging-in-Publication Data

Coulter, Philip B.
  Political voice.

  (ISSR monograph series; no. 1)
  Bibliography: p.
  Includes index.
  1. Municipal services—Alabama—Birmingham—Citizen
participation. 2. Political participation—Alabama—
Birmingham. 3. Municipal government—Information
services—United States. 4. Political participation—
United States. I. Title. II. Series.
HD4606.A4C68   1988   320.8′0973   86-14617
ISBN 0-8173-0338-3

For Greg and Amy

This book was written as a collaborative venture with the Kettering Foundation of Dayton, Ohio. The views contained herein are those of the author and do not necessarily reflect the official position of the Kettering Foundation.

Contents

Tables and Figures

Tables

Figures

Foreword

Cities and their elected officials confront an extraordinary array of challenges in the mid-1980s. These challenges include drastic reductions in federal funding for programs that benefit cities; the need for aging industrial centers such as Birmingham to create and sustain new, more diversified economies; the participation by cities in sophisticated economic development projects as full-fledged members of public-private partnerships; and the continuing objective of fashioning harmonious, multiracial communities. In the midst of these extraordinary challenges, some very old tasks continue to loom large on the municipal agenda. Citizens look to city government to help create and maintain a quality environment where they may work, live, raise families, and pursue cultural and recreational opportunities. Citizens also expect their municipal government to provide an array of public services, equitably and efficiently.

These expectations by citizens frequently lead to complaints. When I first took office in 1979, several members of my staff fielded complaints and attempted to resolve them in cooperation with the staffs of the operating agencies of the city. We quickly concluded that our method of handling complaints was not achieving the desired results, and I established the Mayor's Office of Citizens Assistance with several goals in mind. First, I wanted to establish an easily identified office which citizens could contact with their complaints and requests. Second, I wanted to assemble a small staff committed to providing a courteous response to every citizen who came in, phoned in, or wrote in with a complaint. Third, I was interested in establishing a staff that was knowledgeable enough about city government to refer complaints promptly to the appropriate city agency. Finally, I wanted to establish a systematic procedure for handling each complaint and maintaining a record of activities by this office. In particular, because I knew that citizens will call several different officials with the same complaint in an effort to seek satisfaction, I wanted to be certain we created a system to identify such multiple complaints and thereby increase the efficiency with which city personnel responded.

I was delighted when Dr. Philip Coulter of The University of Alabama expressed an interest in using the Mayor's Office of Citizens Assistance as a research site here in Birmingham. I am equally pleased that his relationship with the city resulted in both a valuable contribution to academic literature and a valuable evaluation of the Mayor's Office of Citizens Assistance.

One of the main strengths of *Political Voice* is Coulter's use of theories of political participation to describe and explain Birmingham's rich experience with citizen contacting of government officials and, conversely, his use of Birmingham's experience to examine and enrich theories of citizen participation. Citizen contacting, like elections, provides an important opportunity for citizens to express their preferences and influence the delivery of basic public services. The City of Birmingham established the Mayor's Office of Citizens Assistance with the intention of strengthening this opportunity. It is gratifying to learn from Coulter's detailed analysis that Birmingham residents have a strong political voice.

In addition to expressing appreciation to Dr. Coulter and his colleagues for this work, I would also like to commend the employees who have served in the Mayor's Office of Citizens Assistance. Dr. Coulter notes that citizens generally evaluated these staff members as "constantly courteous" and that "citizen satisfaction with MOCA was high." I believe we have succeeded in our efforts to create a mechanism that fosters citizen confidence in their government and in their government's interest in responding to their problems.

Richard Arrington, Jr.
Mayor

Birmingham, Alabama

Acknowledgments

I express my appreciation to several people who assisted in the completion of this monograph. James Barnard, Timothy Barnes, Renee Collier, Byron Findley, Gigi Folsom, Richard Mink, and Samuel Fisher, research assistants in the University of Alabama's Institute for Social Science Research, helped collect the data. Edward Lamonte, Leonard Gedgoudas, and Jacqueline Belcher, members of Birmingham Mayor Richard Arrington's staff, generously provided access to municipal archives. Frank Blitz and Robert Luskin of the University of Alabama, Jeffrey L. Brudney of the University of Georgia, John Clayton Thomas of the University of Missouri, Kansas City, and Rodney Hero of the University of Colorado in Colorado Springs read all or parts of the manuscript and made many helpful comments that led to an improved final draft. Sue Freeman and Ginger Kicker typed several editions of the manuscript with skill and speed. Don A. Newton, Jr., staff photographer for the Birmingham Area Chamber of Commerce, supplied the photograph of the Birmingham cityscape that appears on the front cover. The book could not have been written without the contributions of all these people. I accept full responsibility for any errors of fact or interpretation.

Political Voice

1
Contacting as Political Participation

Political participation is usually defined as "acts that aim at *influencing* the government, either by affecting the choice of government personnel or by affecting the *choices made* by government personnel" (Verba and Nie, 1972:2). Participatory acts directed toward influencing the choice of government personnel, for example, voting in elections and campaign activity, have traditionally received scholarly attention (Campbell et al., 1960; Milbrath and Goel, 1977).

More recently, political scientists have begun to study the frequency and importance of participatory acts designed to influence choices made by government personnel. A critically important mode of citizen participation in urban political systems is citizen-initiated contact with a government official to request or complain about public services. Hirschman argued that "the performance of a firm or an organization is assumed to be subject to deterioration for unspecified, random causes which are neither so compelling nor so durable as to prevent a return to previous performance levels provided managers direct their energy and attention to that task" (1970:4). Two options are available under this condition. Those who stop buying the firm's product or who leave the organization exercise the "exit" option. Those who express their dissatisfaction and preferences directly to management use the "voice" option. Citizen-initiated contacting is a pure form of Hirschman's "voice" in the political system. This chapter introduces contacting by presenting several reasons for its importance, describing several dimensions of contacting, discussing numerous characteristics of contacting that make it unique, and reviewing the two major modes of studying contact behavior.

1

Importance of Contacting

Citizen-initiated contacts are important primarily because of their relationship to four aspects of democracy: participation, representation, responsiveness, and distributional equity. Maintaining strong direct links between elites and masses in a democracy is critically important. Contacting is as much a form of linkage between political elites and masses as is voting in elections (Vedlitz, Dyer, and Durand, 1980). It is a legitimate mechanism by which any adult citizen may "affect the choices made by government personnel" (Verba and Nie, 1972:2). Furthermore, it perhaps involves people who might not otherwise participate in the political system. If indeed it does so, contacting facilitates support of the political system by citizens who might otherwise remain indifferent and apathetic (Dran and Smith, 1984).

Similarly, contacting involves democratic representation. A "contact is a demand for representation in that the contactor asks in effect that an official act on behalf of his concerns" (Eisinger, 1972:43). In a democracy, citizens confer upon elected officials the authority to act in regard to interests that the citizen is incapable of managing alone. Contacting activates this representational relationship between individual and officialdom.

Participatory and representational aspects of contacting strengthen its ability to make the political system responsive (Jones et al., 1977). Contacting can influence initiation of policies, but its major effect probably relates to adjustment of ongoing policies. Contacting provides feedback from citizens to government about the impact of government practices (Mladenka, 1977). It keeps government responsive by alerting officials to the unintended consequences of policies, operation of bureaucratic routines, and inequities in policy implementation. Citizens can use contacting to evaluate government responsiveness and to control important activities of the political system.

Many citizen-initiated contacts deal with the quality and quantity of municipal services that affect basic aspects of urban residents' environments and lives. These services can be withheld, and much of their nature and quality is determined by bureaucratic policymakers and "street-level bureaucrats" (Lipsky, 1980). As the administrative and regulatory side of government has become increasingly complex and important, bureaucrats have gained discretionary authority (Thomas, 1982). Contacts with bureaucrats have thus become more important, particularly in service areas where an "Adam Smith" decision rule is in effect (Levy, Meltsner, and Wildavsky, 1974), stating that bureaucrats should provide service only to citizens who request it. Such a rule determining who gets what makes citizen initiative in requesting the service absolutely critical to the government's distribution of service among people, places, and groups. Distributional equity of a service can be seriously affected by contacting when an Adam Smith rule is in effect.

Dimensions of Contacting

Contacting has five important dimensions: nature of the contact, substantive content, referent, level of government to which it is directed, and channel or target of the contact (Eisinger, 1972). A review of the conceptual terrain will help clarify the focus and context of the present book.

"Nature of the contact" means whether it is a request or an expression of opinion. There are three separate types of requests: complaints, requests for help, and demands that "something" be done. A citizen can contact an official to complain about some specific problem, for example, mistreatment by a police officer, the failure of a social security check to arrive on time, or a landlord's refusal to provide a customary service. The complainant feels that he/she has suffered or is threatened by some specific intolerable difficulty or injustice. Contactors also ask for help that does not pertain to perceived mistreatment or injustice, perhaps by asking for information or for an ordinary public service to which the contactor feels entitled. Some contactors make a less specific request that an official "do something" about a problem and do not themselves suggest any particular solution. Such a request calls attention to a general problem, such as job discrimination or high unemployment, but proposes no particular course of action. All three types of request contact provide public officials with an opportunity to act, but they differ in terms of specificity of the contactor's preference for action.

Expressions of opinion differ from requests in that the former are reactions to an existing issue rather than personal initiatives taken by a contactor on a problem of his/her selection. Citizens can contact a public authority to support or oppose a specific option with regard to an existing issue or problem among a variety of alternative solutions. Telling a member of Congress to vote for (against) a given piece of legislation or trying to persuade a member of the city council to provide more funding for emergency medical services is an example of an opinion expressed in support of or in opposition to some alternative solution to an issue. A second type of opinion contact involves merely a comment on the status quo or the communication of support or opposition to a public official for action already taken. Expressions of opinion are reactions either to known policy alternatives or to a policy decision that an official has made.

A second major dimension of contacting is the content of the contact, that is, the substance or topic about which a citizen expresses a request or opinion. While the potential variety of such citizen concerns is almost infinite, contacts about the quality and quantity of local public services are probably more frequent. But more general public issues also receive attention, for example, prayer in the public schools and arms control negotiations.

The third dimension, the contact referent, is extremely important. The referent is the entity on whose behalf a contact is made, the entity intended to be the main recipient of benefits resulting from positive government action. Three referents are evident in the urban political system: an individual and his/her family or household, the neighborhood, and the community at large. Some contactors ask government to do something specific for them or complain that something unfair has been done to them or their families. They intend to influence government to act in such a way that they will receive specific, direct benefits from the action. A request that the city demolish an old, abandoned building next door so that the contactor's children will not be injured there would be one sort of narrow- or particularized-referent contact. Sometimes contacts with an individual and his/her family as referents are difficult to distinguish from contacts with the neighborhood as referent. A citizen might demand demolition of an old, abandoned building next door to avoid endangering neighborhood children or to prevent decline in neighborhood property values. The municipality or community provides a broad or general referent. Requests for more stringent air quality control standards or complaints about corruption in government are examples of broad-referent contacting.

It is sometimes difficult to determine whether a given contact is particularized (individual/household and neighborhood) or broad (neighborhood and community). A distinction might be made on the basis of an investigator's judgment as to who would have benefited most if the government had responded positively to the contact. Or an investigator may infer from the nature of the contact whom the contactor had in mind as the chief recipient of benefits of the contact. Or it may be possible to ask a contactor directly who was intended to receive the benefits. Gradations from individual/family to neighborhood to community are subtle, and methods for identifying the referent of a given contact are numerous. Most research on contacting, however, has emphasized the importance of differences between broad- and narrow-referent contacting, because the political theory of participation assigns different causal forces to "parochial" and "societal" participation.

The fourth dimension of contact is level of government. In a federal political system such as the United States, citizens can direct their complaints and requests to one or more of three levels of government—local, state, and national. The decision to contact one level rather than another depends on many factors, but certainly the locus of formal responsibility for the contactor's area of concern or complaint is important. In federal polities, however, the responsibility of government at one level overlaps with that of government at others.

Finally, the target to which the contact is directed is a fifth dimension. Two principal targets are evident—elected and bureaucratic officials. A contactor can select a target on the basis of several factors, including a target's official responsibility for the content of the contact, perceived responsiveness to contacts, and salience to the contactor. Different "channels of contact" are used by different kinds of people, and some citizens perceive no channel of contact at all (Sharp, 1980).

The Uniqueness of Contacting

The characteristics of contacting make it a virtually unique form of political participation, especially in comparison with voting, the most popular and elemental political act. Through contacting, a citizen takes the initiative, in other words, chooses the nature, content, referent, target, level of government, and timing of the contact. Contacting is harder than most participatory acts, because the citizen must take the initiative and make the effort. And because the citizen must set the policy agenda of a contact, the subject matter is automatically important and salient to him/her (Lehnen, 1976; Mladenka, 1977; Vedlitz, Dyer, and Durand, 1980).

A significant amount of contacting is thoroughly instrumental, that is, is intended to elicit specific, narrow, tangible, service-related benefits from government in the immediate future (Thomas, 1982). In the case of such particularized contacting, the outcomes are specific to the individual, household or family, and immediate living area rather than being broad in impact. The method is direct contact with government personnel to influence their actions. Voting, in contrast, is designed to influence the selection of government personnel and is mediated through electoral institutions. As a representational relationship, contacting takes place between citizen and official, not between electorate and legislature (Eisinger, 1972).

Contacting involves the individual in an active "consumer" role rather than in a traditional "citizen" role (Jacob, 1972). It focuses on citizen-government relationships built around government outputs, primarily provision of services and regulation of behavior. As such it constitutes an important feedback mechanism through which citizens can specifically inform government about the extent to which services and regulations accord with their preferences.

Contacting contrasts with other types of political participation in that it involves little direct conflict with other citizens (Verba and Nie, 1972). Generally a particularized contact involves no opposition, no public issue, and no sides to choose between. With these characteristics, contacting tends to put only a low degree of pressure on the contacted official because usually only one citizen makes the request, although the request may be quite specific.

Table 1-1. **Contrasting Characteristics of
Particularized Contacting and Voting**

Aspect	Particularized contacting	Voting
1. Source of initiative[a]	citizen	government
2. Salience of issue(s)	high	low to high
3. Purpose	instrumental	can be noninstrumental
4. Clarity of outcome	unambiguous	usually ambiguous
5. Scope of outcome	narrow	broad
6. Intention of influence	actions of officials	selection of officials
7. Side of political process	output	input
8. Level of conflict	low	low to high
9. Pressure on official	low	high
10. Partisanship	low	usually high
11. Participant's state of mind	primarily dissonant	usually consonant

[a]"Initiative" here is taken to mean determination of the nature, content, referent, target, level of government, and timing of participation.

Contacting is disaggregated and low pressure rather than aggregated but vague, as elections are. Furthermore, contacting seems to fit the old adage in municipal government: "There is no Republican way to pave a street and no Democratic way to cover a manhole." Contacting is nonpartisan. Finally, a contact indicates dissatisfaction, even some mild anger, strong enough to produce complaint behavior; a contactor is in a dissonant state of mind. The voter's state of mind is more consonant, more in harmony with the political system. Table 1-1 summarizes the eleven ways in which particularized contacting contrasts with voting as a mode of political participation.

Collecting Data

The present book is concerned with all local government contacts, but its primary focus is particularized contacts with local government bureaucratic officials. All such contacts are considered, without regard to their content. Similarly, local government contacts of any nature are included, regardless of whether they are requests or expressions of opinion. By restricting the analysis to local government contacts, however, I naturally homogenize target, referent, content, and nature of contacting to some extent. Researchers use two methods to identify a contact and to determine its nature, content, referent, level of government, and target. The first is survey research, a microanalytic method. Adult respondents can be asked, in a random sample survey, whether they have contacted a government official and numerous other questions that describe the various dimensions of contacting and the contactor. Individual citizens are the unit of analysis. The second research method is macroanalytic and uses official government records. Agency archives can be sampled for the names and addresses of persons who have contacted the agency to express an opinion or make a request. The address makes it possible to locate the contactor in his/her census tract or other subarea of the city. When these individual contacts are aggregated to the level of census tracts, tracts become the unit of analysis. Contacting is measured as a geographical phenomenon, for example, number of contacts per 1,000 population in each of the tracts. Numerous other social and demographic characteristics of the tracts can be obtained from U.S. Census reports.

Each method has advantages and disadvantages. Survey research is certainly a better way to measure demographic, social, political, and attitudinal characteristics of contactors. A representative sample, however, is likely to contain too few contactors for analysis, relies on sometimes faulty recall of respondents, and provides no information about the government response to contact. The use of aggregate data from government records does not depend on respondents' recall, and the government's response to contacts can be documented. The use of aggregate data, however, does not permit individual demographic, social, political, or attitudinal data to be linked with contacting. Inferences about the way individuals behave from the behavior of census tracts may be fallacious. And sometimes government records can be faulty; for example, it is unlikely that any agency actually records all of its citizen-initiated contacts (Jones, 1980:52–53).

Procedure

Chapter 1 sets the stage by introducing contacting as an important, multidimensional, unique act of political participation in a democracy. Chapter 2 reviews and synthesizes the scholarly literature on citizen-initiated contacting and explains who contacts and why. Several explanatory models of contacting are identified in terms of the hypothesized relationship between contacting and socioeconomic status (SES), certain participatory civic attitudes, need for government services, and race. The literature manifests considerable disagreement as to which model best explains contacting, and the conclusion of chapter 2 explores several reasons for these disagreements. In addition to identifying the major models of contacting, chapter 2 also discusses the estimated rates of contacting reported in numerous studies and the kinds of problems about which people initiate contacts.

Chapter 3 tests the several models of contacting with data from the city of Birmingham, Alabama. Archival contact data, collected from the Birmingham Mayor's Office of Citizens Assistance (MOCA) and aggregated to the census tract level, are subjected to multiple regression analysis. None of the models identified in the literature provides a satisfactory explanation of contacting in Birmingham. Empirical analysis of the Birmingham data leads to development of a new model and also suggests that we need to rethink various theoretical assumptions about the relationships between socioeconomic status, civic attitudes, need for government services, and race.

Chapter 3 also explores contactors' satisfaction with the government's response to their contacts as revealed by data collected in a survey of a random sample of Birmingham residents who contacted the Mayor's Office of Citizens Assistance. Despite the fact that most contacts are at least in part complaints, so that contactors are complainers, most express considerable satisfaction with both the process and the outcome of their contacts.

Chapter 4 returns to a theme first introduced in chapter 1, namely that contacting is a relatively unique form of political participation, with the implication that contactors are significantly different from other citizens. This chapter tests several hypotheses drawn from the literature that addresses this question, that is, whether contactors tend to engage only in contacting or participate in a variety of political activities. A comparison of data from the survey of Birmingham contactors and data from a survey of Birmingham's adult residents indicates that the model of contactors on which most studies explicitly or implicitly draw is by no means universally accurate. Birmingham's contactors do not fit the mold. The final chapter reanalyzes the major models of contacting, in particular, contact theory and methodology. Much of the research on contacting rests on assumptions about the relationships of need for government services and participatory civic attitudes with socioeconomic status. Both a review of previous findings and the results of analyzing contacts in Birmingham strongly indicate that we need to rethink the prevalent assumptions. The assumptions underlying most models cannot be consistently confirmed, and chapter 5 offers a new perspective on contact theory.

Another theme introduced in chapter 1—whether contact data are collected from survey research or from government records—is further developed in the final chapter. The evidence suggests that the way contacting is studied—whether by microanalysis of survey data or by macroanalysis of aggregate data—influences conclusions as to which model best explains contact behavior. Further study of contacting should preclude the risks of producing methodological artifacts as conclusions, and this final chapter suggests a research design that can provide more reliable and valid conclusions. The chapter ends with final observations about contacting in Birmingham and about the causal forces underlying contacting.

2
Models of Contacting:

Who, Why, about What, and How Often?

Who initiates contacts with municipal officials? Why do they do so? The two questions are closely related. In fact, the theories of why people contact or what motivates them to do so rest largely on various characteristics of the contactors themselves. Several conflicting theories of citizen-initiated contacting abound in the research literature. This chapter reviews and evaluates various empirical studies that have attempted to verify one explanatory model or another. We will first consider the frequency with which citizens contact in American cities and the content of contacts.

The Rate of Contacting

Local government contacting has been studied through the use of survey research in over a dozen American cities, three times in U.S. national samples, and several times in foreign cities, provinces, or countries. Investigators can, using this microanalytic technique for the collection of data, derive estimates of the overall contact rate among adults in the municipal or national population. Although respondents' recall may be faulty, survey research is probably the best method by which to estimate contact rates for a population.

It is well known that *how* a survey asks a question may influence the kinds of answers it elicits. This principle no doubt applies to questions about contacting local public officials. The point is important, because investigators have asked the question in a variety of ways, and contact rate estimates could in part be an artifact of question wording.

Variety in the wording of contact questions is worthy of brief discussion. Eisinger, in explaining the survey instrument he used to study Milwaukee, said: "Respondents were asked if, 'within the last couple of years,' they had personally written a letter, sent a telegram, or spoken to any of a variety of different types of public officials on a list which was handed to them. These officials ranged from the President of the United States to the mayor of Milwaukee to 'any person at all who works for the City of Milwaukee'" (1972:45).

By presenting respondents with a list of officials, the survey could have stimulated recall that might otherwise have remained dormant. Also, the question allowed respondents to recall any contacts within the past two years. Thomas's survey of Cincinnati residents included a similarly broad question. His "measure of citizen-initiated contact is based on a question asked separately for *each of the ten service areas,* on whether the respondents or *any other members of their households* had called the department or division in the past year with a request for service or a complaint" (1982:507; italics added). This question possibly stimulated recall with a list of municipal agencies and encompassed the respondent and all other members of his/her household but restricted the time period of contact to one year.

Another approach, that preferred by Sharp in her study of Wichita, made no attempt to stimulate recall with mention of particular target agencies or officials but considerably expanded the time horizon and included "government issues" as content: "Contacting behavior is measured by a yes-no survey item asking whether the respondent has *ever* contacted a local public official about a government issue or community problem" (1982:110; italics added).

Brown's study of Kitchener, Ontario, Canada, constrained the time period and mentioned no targets but did suggest alternative natures of the contact: "Specifically, respondents were asked whether in the past year, they could recall wanting to contact local officials to complain about something, to request information, or to render an opinion on some matter. If respondents would recall such an occasion, they were invited to describe the nature of the matter and were asked whether in fact they had contacted someone about it" (1982:220).

Table 2-1. **Estimated Local Government Contact Rates in Various Political Jurisdictions**

City	Overall contact rate	Contact time period	Particularized-contact rate[a]
1. Cincinnati (Thomas, 1982)	55[b]	past year	N/A
2. Springfield, Ill. (Shin and Everson, 1980)	47	past year	"lion's share"
3. Garland, Tex. (Vedlitz and Veblen, 1980)	44	ever	>50
4. U.S.A.[c] (Steger, Vertz, and Wirth, 1982)	41	ever	N/A
5. Decatur, Ill. (Shin and Everson, 1980)	38	past year	"lion's share"
6. Peoria, Ill. (Shin and Everson, 1980)	35	past year	"lion's share"
7. Colorado Springs (Hero, 1986)	35	N/A	N/A
8. East St. Louis, Mo. (Altes and Mendelson, 1980)	31	past year	N/A
9. U.S.A. (Lehnen, 1976)	30	ever	N/A
10. Detroit (Dran and Smith, 1984)	28	ever	>56
11. Kansas City, Kans. (Sharp, 1984a)	28	past year	31
12. Wichita, Kans. (Sharp, 1982)	25	ever	N/A
13. Kitchener, Ontario, Canada (Brown, 1982)	24	past year	92
14. Milwaukee, Wis. (Eisinger, 1972)	23[b]	past two years	83
15. United States (Verba and Nie, 1972)	20	ever	35
16. Alberta, Canada (Friedman, 1974)	15/21	ever	N/A
17. Britain (Friedman, 1974)	17	ever	N/A

Note: Figures in cells are percentages. N/A = not available.
[a]Percentage of contactors whose referent was particularized.
[b]Respondent or anyone in the household and specified government agencies or officials.
[c]Sample includes all central cities only.

Table 2-1 presents estimated contact rates for several American cities, for the United States in three separate studies, and for several foreign political jurisdictions, drawing on survey research employing variously worded questions. Estimated overall contact rates vary widely, from a low of 20 percent in Verba and Nie's (1972) U.S. national survey to a high of 55 percent in Thomas's (1982) survey of Cincinnati. The mean rate is 33 percent, and the median is 30 percent. It seems to make no consistent difference whether a question stimulated recall with mention of numerous specific targets; whether it included one, two, or all past years; whether it included only the respondent or all members of the household; or whether it referred to a particular nature or particular content of contacts. A much larger number of examples would be necessary to determine the impact of question wording definitively. However, it certainly seems possible that variously worded survey questions of individuals provide contact rate estimates whose validity and reliability invite scrutiny.

The estimated rate of contacts for the United States citizenry provides a useful illustration. Steger, Vertz, and Wirth (1982), analyzing a central city subsample of 2,969 respondents drawn from a national survey conducted by the U.S. Department of Housing and Urban Development, found a 41 percent contact rate. Lehnen's (1976) national sample showed a 30 percent contact rate. Verba and Nie's (1972) national sample indicated that 20 percent of all adult Americans have contacted a local government official. A difference as large as 10 percent between two large national samples is unlikely to occur by chance. A difference as large as 20 percent is truly a statistical phenomenon. Estimates with such large differences in size could be expected to differ in socioeconomic characteristics as well. What accounts for the difference? The questions were identical in wording.

In a similar vein, compare each of the individual city contact rates with that of U.S. central cities as estimated by Steger, Vertz, and Wirth (1982). All the cities except Garland, Texas, are central cities, but most of them have contact rates significantly below the U.S. central-city estimate of 41 percent. The precision of these estimates is open to question. There might be intercity differences that can account for the wide variance in contact rates. I review these differences later in the chapter.

Discrepancies among estimates of particularized contacting rates are also noteworthy. Table 2-1 includes a few estimates of the percentage of all local government contacts that had particularized referents. They range from a low of 31 percent in Kansas City to a high of 92 percent in Kitchener, Canada. In fact, only Sharp's (1984a) Kansas City estimate and Verba and Nie's (1972) national estimate are below 50 percent (31 percent and 35 percent, respectively). All others reported are much higher, although many investigators did not report percentage of particularized contacts. One can only tentatively conclude that estimates of both local government contacting and particularized contacting rates vary substantially among American cities and from sample to sample in the nation as a whole. The reasons for this variance are not obvious.

The Content of Contacting

Citizen-initiated contacting reflects numerous problems that relate to a variety of municipal services. These problems and the services provided to alleviate them seriously affect the quality of life available to residents of each neighborhood in a city. Some contacting studies specifically identified the content that prompts such political participation. It is possible to compare more or less common categories of contact content from several municipalities for the sake of understanding why citizens initiate contact.

Table 2-2 lists the more popular reasons why citizens contact local government officials. The list is incomplete and contains some blank cells; to go any farther would require us to compare categories that are probably incomparable, because different researchers categorized contacts differently. Table 2-2 presents conservative estimates of citizens' concerns when initiating a contact.

The largest category of complaints includes overgrown vacant lots, debris, dead trees and tree limbs, and so forth, cases that are clearly examples of environmental negative externalities. Such negative externalities can be caused either by private citizens (e.g., the owner of a vacant lot who fails to keep it cleared) or by government action (e.g., municipal street-paving crews who leave debris in a citizen's yard). The second most popular subject of contact concerns streets and sidewalks, almost exclusively a public sector responsibility. Complaints regarding potholes, broken sidewalks,

Table 2-2. **Content of Citizen-Initiated Contacts (percent)**

	Kitchener[a]	Garland[b]	Dallas[c]	Houston[c]	Houston[d]	Cincinnati[e]	Detroit[f]	Birmingham[g]
1. Overgrowth, debris	6.2	13.5	25.9	27.9	27.0	13.6	37.8	34.1
2. Streets, sidewalks	20.4	8.7	9.5	20.8	8.7	21.1	8.4	27.5
3. Drainage, flooding	10.6	6.7	19.3	34.7	22.5	—	3.8	5.5
4. Building code violations	—	3.8	13.3	2.8	—	8.0	8.9	11.5
5. Animal control	8.8	8.7	11.8	6.9	4.8	—	—	4.1
6. Police and fire	2.7	4.8	4.7	0.6	—	32.0	3.8	1.5
7. Parks and recreation	6.2	1.9	—	—	—	6.5	—	0.1

Note: Columns do not sum to 100 because list is incomplete.
[a]Brown (1982).
[b]Vedlitz and Veblen (1980).
[c]Vedlitz, Dyer, and Durand (1980).
[d]Mladenka (1977).
[e]Thomas (1982).
[f]Bachelor (1983).
[g]See chapter 3.

and traffic control signs that are missing or needed dominate this category. Some complaints regarding overgrowth and debris have private solutions; complaints about streets and sidewalks almost always require public solutions.

The third category of contacts pertains to drainage, sewer, flooding, and related water problems, another set of environmental complaints that affects the quality of residents' housing. The fourth most frequent type of complaint, building code violations, is similar. It includes citizens' requests that the city enforce rental housing regulations and do something about abandoned buildings. Abandoned structures are neighborhood eyesores; they also house rodents and are potentially dangerous to children. In either case, they are likely to depress property values. Mentioned with almost equal frequency is the problem of animal control, in other words, stray dogs running loose in the neighborhood. This problem, like those in most of the other categories, concerns environmental health, safety, aesthetics, and, therefore, property values.

Cities' percentages in each of the categories of contact content shown in table 2-2 display fairly wide dispersion. Birmingham's percentages seem to be consistent with those of the other larger cities in the table.

Who Contacts? Socioeconomic Status, Civic Attitudes, Need, and Race

The relationship between socioeconomic status and political participation has a special place in social science. This fairly strong positive association has been confirmed literally thousands of times in studies of American politics and of foreign political systems as well (Almond and Verba, 1965; Milbrath and Goel, 1977). Naturally, when scholars began to study citizen-initiated contacting, they assumed that the same almost lawlike regularity would prevail—that is, people of higher SES would have a greater propensity to contact. Early studies of contacting employed what is known as the "standard socioeconomic model" (Verba and Nie, 1972).

Verba and Nie stated the case well: "Citizens of higher social and economic status participate more in politics" (1972:125). It is not the higher socioeconomic status per se that increases the tendency to participate in politics; rather it is the civic orientations or attitudes and skills conducive to successful participation that accompany higher SES. People of higher SES, according to the argument, are generally found to exhibit five specific civic orientations that contribute to their higher levels of participation: greater psychological involvement in politics, sense of civic duty, sense of civic efficacy, belief in government responsiveness, and political cognition (Verba and Nie, 1972:133).

"Psychological involvement in politics" refers to citizens' expressed level of interest in and attention to politics. Individuals with higher SES have greater interest and attention levels than persons with low SES. "Sense of civic duty" incorporates the individual's conception of his/her contribution to the community or obligation to the body politic. Citizens with a high sense of civic duty feel an obligation to vote in elections because it is the moral duty of a responsible citizen to do so. Persons of higher SES tend to have a stronger sense of civic duty to participate in local political affairs.

"Sense of civic efficacy" involves the individual's feelings of competence to act politically, in other words, to perform a political activity effectively. "Sense of government responsiveness" indicates the individual's attitude about the extent to which government officials would pay attention to and cooperate with the individual if he/she participated in political activity. Citizens with higher SES tend to have stronger feelings of individual civic efficacy and government responsiveness. Finally, "political cognition" includes the knowledge necessary for political activity, such as the procedure for registering and voting, the name and address of one's state representative or representative to Congress, or the fact that the county sheriff's office (not the city police department) is responsible for law enforcement in one's residential area. People of higher SES usually also have a greater store of information about politics and government in general and are better able to make sense of it.

Persons with higher SES have more political motivation, skills, and resources with which to participate in politics because of their civic orientations. For these reasons, they participate more frequently and successfully. Most researchers have used income, education, and occupation, singly or in combination, to measure SES. For example, persons with higher income could be expected to engage in acts of political participation more frequently than those whose income is lower.

Different investigators discovered different, sometimes contradictory findings using this model to explain contacting, and soon an alternative model emerged. It is known as the "need-awareness" model and posits that people who need government services more and have a greater awareness of how and whom to contact will have a greater propensity to contact. In addition, this model posits that need and awareness each bear a special association with SES. Many other studies have emphasized some derivative or variation of one or the other of these two basic models. Both of these two explanations for contacting as political participation have been widely used by those investigating the subject. Their findings relating SES and contacting are diverse, as figure 2-1 shows: a null or negligible, positive linear, negative linear, and downward-opening curvilinear relationship.

A NEGLIGIBLE OR NULL RELATIONSHIP

Verba and Nie (1972), in their large-scale, comprehensive national study of American political participation, found only a very weak positive relationship between particularized contacting and either SES or any of the intervening civic orientations. They concluded that particularized contacting "derives from a process quite different from the one that leads to other activities" (Verba and Nie, 1972:135). They found that other political activities, such as voting, participation in election campaigns, participation in organizations with political agendas, and general-referent contacting, could be reasonably well explained with the standard socioeconomic model. Thus particularized contacting was dramatically isolated as a type of political activity, different from all others and virtually impossible to explain.

Other investigators have also found negligible or null relationships between SES and particularized contacting. Jacob (1972), in his study of contacting in Milwaukee, found strong racial

Figure 2-1. Models of Citizen-Initiated Contacting

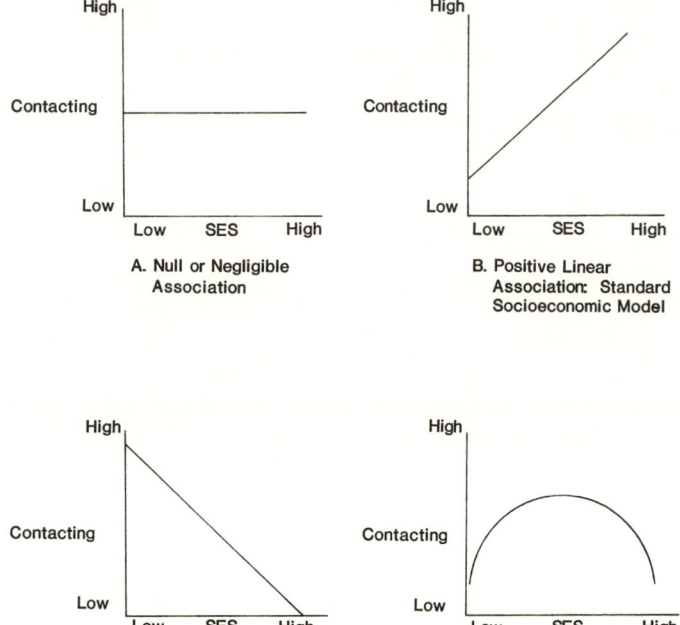

A. Null or Negligible
   Association

B. Positive Linear
   Association: Standard
   Socioeconomic Model

C. Negative Linear
   Association: Need
   Model

D. Curvilinear Associa-
   tion: Need–Awareness
   Model

influences on contacting propensity but virtually no relationship between SES and contacting. Jacob's survey asked respondents about contacts with a specific list of forty-five local government offices and agencies and classified them into six functional categories—for example, regulatory agencies, health agencies, and recreation agencies. He found little or no difference in contact rates between a white working-class sample and a white middle-class sample.

Mladenka (1977) presented a still stronger case that SES does not influence particularized contacting in his research on Houston, using aggregate data collected from the official records of Houston's centralized complaint bureau, the Action Center. His research used census tracts as the unit of analysis and employed percentage black, percentage Chicano, and average value of owner-occupied housing units as independent variables to explain the variation in contact rates among census tracts. He concluded unequivocally that "the evidence suggests that the *level* of contacting does not vary on the basis of socioeconomic status and race" (Mladenka, 1977:285). In other words, rich, middle-class, and poor neighborhoods as well as black, white, and Chicano neighborhoods exhibited approximately the same propensity to contact.

Hero (1986), in a study of Colorado Springs, Colorado, based on survey data, found a null relationship between income and contacting in both univariate and multivariate analyses. His research produced Pearson's simple correlation coefficients of .03 or less between income and several types of contacting. Hero's multivariate discriminant function analysis—statistically appropriate, since the dependent variable is a dichotomous contact or no contact— yielded similar results. Income was nonsignificant when the impact of perceived need, age, and race was controlled.

Friedman (1974:35–38) found primarily very weak relationships between several indexes of SES and contacting in his study of Great Britain and Canada's Alberta Province, based on survey research. When he cross-tabulated SES and complaining, all seven relationships were statistically significant, but their average Cramer's *V* measure of association was only .14. Friedman calls this "a fairly clear indication that socio-economic factors are associated with the decision to complain" (1974:35), but these coefficient values are more accurately interpreted as indicating a negligible relationship. Similarly, four separate measures of SES demonstrated only a slight relationship to political efficacy in both countries, with Kentall's tau_c coefficients of association ranging from .13 to .22. In any case, it is clear that, in Britain and Alberta, socioeconomic status explains neither contacting nor efficacy.

In her study of Kansas City, Sharp (1984b) also found the socioeconomic explanation inadequate. She separately identified particularized and general-referent contactors by asking respondents who had contacted whether they had done so about something concerning themselves or their family or about something of

concern to the community in general. In both cases, the gamma
association with income and education varied from .09 to .14,
hardly a serious relationship (Sharp, 1984b:33). Her analysis
showed that socioeconomic status has similarly weak associations
with political efficacy and interest in local government and only a
moderate relationship with knowledge or awareness about government. Both knowledge and interest in government, however, had
only modest gamma association with contacting (γ = .23 and .24,
respectively). Political efficacy did have a fairly strong relationship
with contacting (γ = .43), but we should recall that efficacy was
only quite weakly associated with SES (Sharp, 1984b:36).

Sharp's explanation of the failure of the standard socioeconomic
model is important. She argued that the SES model fails to explain
contacting of local government officials because citizen orientations toward the urban political system differ considerably from
orientations toward the American national political system (Sharp,
1984b:38). She reasoned that because municipal government is
close to the citizen and delivers services directly and daily, citizens
have an "entitlement" orientation toward local government—that
is, they feel entitled to consume the services that local government
produces and have a clear feeling about what these services should
be. An ethic of self-reliance characterizes orientations of both dis-
advantaged and advantaged citizens toward national government;
they feel that they should take care of almost any problem, personal
or social, without help from government (Brody and Sniderman,
1977; Sharp 1984b).

A POSITIVE LINEAR RELATIONSHIP: THE STANDARD SES MODEL

Investigators who have found a negligible or null association
between SES and contacting are in a distinct minority. Many others
have confirmed the basic validity of the standard socioeconomic
model and defended contacting as a typical mode of political participation. Surveys of contacting in nine American cities, in the
United States, and in foreign countries indicate a moderate or
strong positive association. Eisinger's (1972) research on contacting in Milwaukee produced findings that contrast with those of

Jacob (1972) on the same city. For a random sample of 495 Milwaukee adults, Eisinger found that "the gamma correlation between education and contact for whites is .46, while for blacks it
rises to .70. Income and contact are related for blacks (.47), but not
for whites" (1972:47). Clearly, contactors were identified as better
off than noncontactors in terms of social well-being.

The results of Shin and Everson's (1980) study of Springfield,
Decatur, and Peoria, three middle-sized Illinois cities, contrast
with those of Verba and Nie's national survey. Shin and Everson
found persons of higher income and high school education to be
significantly overrepresented among contactors. Another strong
confirmation of the SES model is a study by Vedlitz and Veblen
(1980), who found a significant moderate gamma association (γ =
.28) between education and contacting for all respondents in
Garland, Texas. Even when the effect of level of political interest
was controlled, the relationship between education and contacting
remained significant. Political interest, the "intervening" civic orientation, seemed not to intervene in the Garland, Texas, study.

Brown (1982), studying Kitchener, Ontario, Canada, found a
significant gamma association of .36 between respondents' education level and their contacting. Of perhaps more importance is his
observation that, although "contacting would seem to be at least
partially a function of SES as measured by the respondent's education level . . . , the nature of this relationship is not well specified
by the (four) civic orientations" (Brown, 1982:224). Brown examined the SES-contacting relationship when controlling, respectively, for political efficacy, interest, involvement, and awareness.
He found that it changed only slightly. Three of the gamma coefficients relating civic orientations to both SES and contacting were
not statistically significant. The other five were considerably
smaller than that between SES and contacting. Brown's research,
like that of Vedlitz and Veblen, seems to indicate that the standard
socioeconomic model might be reasonably accurate but perhaps
not for the conventionally accepted reason. That is, higher SES
might not necessarily produce civic orientations that prompt citizens to engage in greater contacting.

Sharp's (1982) study of contacting in Wichita essentially confirmed the SES model. She emphatically observed that some ear-

lier findings (e.g., the national sample survey of Verba and Nie, 1972), were concerned only with particularized contacting. In this context, she argued: "It is possible that subtracting all broad-referent contacts from the dependent variable may mask a relationship between contacting in general and socioeconomic status, especially if the broad-referent component is very strongly and positively associated with SES" (Sharp, 1982:110). She found a gamma coefficient of association of .47 between SES and contact behavior. In line with the concept of civic orientations, she also found that political efficacy is fairly strongly related to both SES and contacting but that, even when the influence of efficacy was controlled, a strong relationship remained between SES and contacting.

Steger, Vertz, and Wirth (1982), in a large national study based on survey data from U.S. central cities, focused on "problem-solving participation," a category that included both broad- and particularized-referent contacting as well as neighborhood cooperative activity. The latter included working with others, forming a group to work on local problems, and active membership in community problem-solving organizations. Contacting and cooperative activity are both instrumental activities, require considerable individual initiative, and could involve a collective outcome, since contacting can have a social referent, and cooperative activity is directed toward solution of social problems (Steger, Vertz, and Wirth, 1982:5).

Steger, Vertz, and Wirth's national study concluded: "There is a positive, linear relationship between SES and problem-solving participation even when controls are imposed for the interaction of need and perceived responsiveness" (Steger, Vertz, and Wirth, 1982:13). But even with a Pearson's simple correlation coefficient of .33, the authors of this study surmised "that the SES model of participation is not entirely satisfactory" (1982:18). Yet they found SES to be the best explanatory variable among the several they used.

Dran and Smith (1984), in a survey of Detroit, separated "issue" contacting (similar to social-referent contacting) from "particularized" contacting. One question asked respondents about contacting a local government official to express their views on some issue, and another asked if they had contacted a local official to complain about some service. The authors used several variables to explain both types of contact propensity and concluded that "the analysis of issue contacting indicates that SES is the most influential of the explanatory variables in accounting for this act" (Dran and Smith, 1984:23). Surprisingly, they also concluded that "SES continues to exert a significant direct and indirect effect upon particularized contacting" (Dran and Smith, 1984:24), although they found two other variables (awareness and need) to be slightly more important.

A NEGATIVE LINEAR RELATIONSHIP: NEED ONLY

Several studies defended the model that posits a moderate-to-strong, positive linear association between socioeconomic status and contacting. Several other studies tested the model and found only negligible or null relationships. One quite rigorous macro-analysis of contacting in Houston and Dallas found a fairly strong *negative* linear relationship. Vedlitz, Dyer, and Durand (1980) examined contacts with both cities' centralized complaint centers using multiple regression analysis. Average value of renter-occupied housing, median family income, and age of housing each explained from 53 percent to 88 percent of the variance in contacting among Houston neighborhoods and up to 42 percent of contacting in Dallas. The relationship was negative, however. Citizens of higher-income areas tended to contact less; low-income areas produced more contacts. Presumably, lower SES meant greater need for government service, which yielded a greater propensity to contact.

Burnett, Cole, and Moon (1983) found a similar relationship between need and contacting in their aggregate data study of Portsmouth, England. They regressed housing complaints on indexes of housing deterioration and awareness for 277 enumeration districts. Level of housing need produced a significant positive coefficient, but awareness was negative and nonsignificant.

Haeberle (1986) studied "requests for city action" submitted by elective neighborhood organization leaders to the Birmingham, Alabama, Department of Community Development. Almost cer-

tainly most of those requests originated with citizens as complaints
to their neighborhood leaders. Haeberle discovered that income
had a very strong and significant negative effect on requests (with a
standardized regression coefficient of $-.59$), even when environmental, racial, participatory, and other socioeconomic variables
were controlled in a multiple regression equation. He found that
need for government services predominated, a theme that I will
modify and elaborate in chapter 3.

A CURVILINEAR ASSOCIATION: THE NEED-AWARENESS MODEL

Jones et al. (1980), in their large-scale study of contacting in
Detroit, first recognized the importance of the unique properties of
contacting as an act of political participation. On the basis of their
conception of contacting as a decidedly instrumental form of participation, they developed a different theory to explain it. In the
urban context, they argued, citizens contact their local government
because they need some type of public service. A citizen who feels
no need for the government's services is unlikely to initiate a contact. One of the major reasons for contacting is the existence of
negative externalities in urban neighborhoods produced either by
private citizens' action or by government action. As we have seen,
table 2-2 presented several categories of contacts involving citizens' complaints about such negative externalities, for example,
an absentee landlord who allows his rental property to fall into
disrepair in violation of municipal housing codes.

A citizen, in order to initiate a contact, must also have sufficient
awareness of the political system to do so. Jones et al. (1980:43)
argued that awareness involves four important components. First,
the citizen must be aware that government is legally responsible for
dealing with the problem at hand—that the government actually
provides some service that could be delivered to solve the problem
or ameliorate the citizen's need. Second, the citizen must feel that
the government agency can be persuaded to act—to produce and
deliver the relevant service. Third, the citizen must believe that he/
she can cause government to produce and deliver the service.
Fourth, Jones et al. defined political awareness to include posses-
sion of a channel of influence that the citizen can use to contact

government effectively (see also Sharp, 1980). The concept of "awareness," then, includes political cognition, government responsiveness, efficacy, and a channel of contact.

Jones and associates developed the argument that need for government services is inversely related and awareness positively related to SES or social well-being. The lower the SES of a neighborhood, for example, the greater the intensity of negative externalities such as crime and housing dilapidation, the greater the need for ameliorating public services, and the greater the propensity of its residents to contact local government. The higher the status of a neighborhood, the greater the likelihood that its residents have a contact channel, information, and a high sense of political efficacy and government responsiveness. No matter how great a citizen's need, contact is highly improbable, however, if he/she has no awareness of government. Jones et al. concluded, therefore, that *some* need and *some* awareness must be present to produce a contact. Persons with high need but low awareness and persons with high awareness but low need are less likely to contact government than residents with moderate need and moderate awareness because it is the *interaction* of need and awareness that generates contacts.

As SES increases, need declines and awareness increases. This tendency complicates the relationship between SES and contacting. The result of the theory of Jones et al. is a parabolic or curvilinear relationship between SES and contacting; as SES increases, contacting increases but only up to a point. As SES continues to increase past that point, contacting begins to decrease. Contact propensity, then, is greatest for middle SES and lowest for lower and higher status residents. Figure 2-2 illustrates this complex set of relationships.

Jones et al. examined 2,368 citizen contacts concerning environmental enforcement problems that were processed by the Detroit City Clerk's Office. They geocoded these contacts to Detroit's 420 census tracts, which were the units of analysis. To explain variance in propensity to contact among census tracts, Jones et al. used three census tract characteristics as independent variables: average age of housing structures, percentage black, and distance from the center of the central business district. The latter variable was

Figure 2-2. The Need-Awareness Model

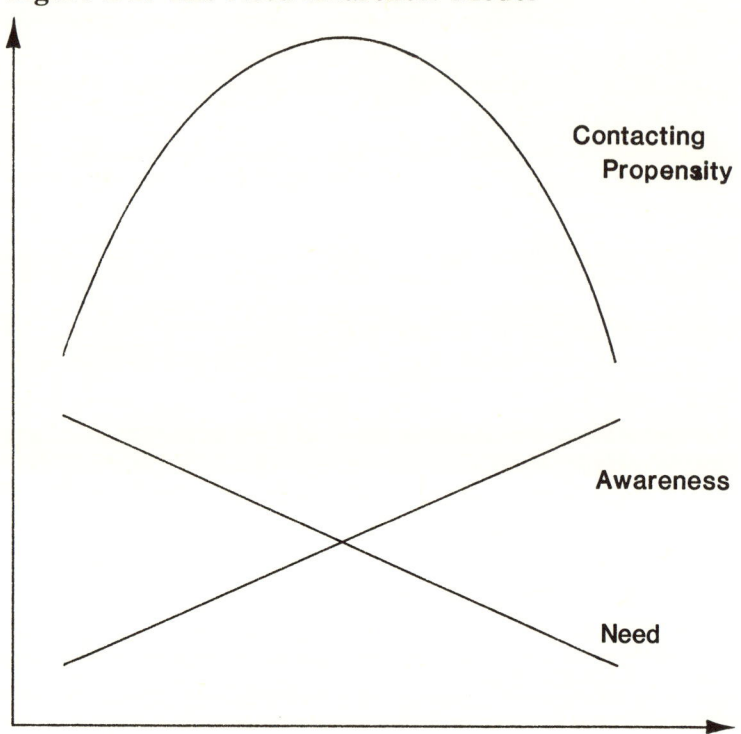

Social Well–Being

used as a general surrogate for social well-being, since Detroit developed according to a "concentric ring model," in which greater distance from the center indicated higher education and income levels and so forth. The researchers found that neighborhoods in the middle range of social well-being had a higher propensity to contact than those at the lower or upper extremes. In other words, they found a parabolic relationship between social well-being and contacting rather than a null, positive linear, or negative linear association. Jones et al. concluded: "First, the findings concerning the generation of citizen contacts support the theory developed in this paper that such contacts, when they concern governmental programs or services which confer particularistic benefits, are a multiplicative function of need for the service and awareness that government is relevant for the amelioration of that need. Need and awareness are assumed to be linearly related to social well-being, the former inversely, the latter directly" (1977:164). Detroit instituted a new centralized complaint office about one year after the Jones et al. project collected data from the city clerk. Bachelor (1983) examined patterns of contacting in Detroit during an eleven-year period after the opening of that new office and generally confirmed the need-awareness model. She observed that "higher proportions of complaints (were) generated by neighborhoods in the middle of the income scale ($10,000 to $14,000) than in lower or higher income areas" (Bachelor, 1983:6). She also concluded that the Detroit data provide "little support for the standard socioeconomic model" (Bachelor, 1983:13).

Many of the studies cited earlier whose findings support a negligible, positive, or negative association between SES and contacting also specifically tested the parabolic need-awareness model but found little or no evidence to confirm it. Some, such as Brown (1982) in his research on Kitchener, Canada, found that need was unrelated to either education or awareness. Others, such as Sharp (1982) in her study of Wichita, found that, although need and awareness were related to SES as postulated, SES maintained a strong association with contacting even when need and awareness were controlled.

THE CLIENTELE NEED MODEL

After the Jones et al. study supporting a curvilinear model had been published, several scholars examined the concept of need more closely. Thomas (1982), for example, argued for a "clientele participation model." In this model, it is assumed that SES and need have a null relationship. People at different levels of SES have different kinds of needs for government services, but all have about the same number of needs. Citizens at different levels of SES who have different kinds of needs contact different government agencies and thus become part of the "clienteles" of different agencies. Thomas's analysis further supported the conclusion that, for a sample of citizens with an equal amount of need, those with higher

SES are more likely to contact government. In other words, need is primary and SES secondary in importance as explanations of contacting.

Brown (1982), similarly, found that Kitchener citizens with low need tend to contact at low rates regardless of their level of awareness and that those with high need tend to contact at two or three times the other group's rate, regardless of their level of awareness. He found that for moderate-need citizens, however, as awareness increased, so did propensity to contact. In other words, awareness really counts only for citizens of moderate need. Steger, Vertz, and Wirth drew essentially the same conclusion when they stated: "We are suggesting that there may be different models of problem-solving participation for different levels of socioeconomic status. Factors of area need and efficacy may take on different meanings for individuals of high, medium, and low SES levels (1982:23).

Dran and Smith's (1984) work essentially agreed with Thomas's (1982) conclusions about the primacy of need. They analyzed general-issue contacting and particularized contacting separately on the basis of a survey of Detroit residents that included questions designed to measure need separately for each type of contact. Citizens who could mention a local issue facing the community that could be addressed by local government were classified as having an issue need; those who could think of no such issue were coded as having no such need. Similarly, respondents whose answers to questions about five city services indicated that they were satisfied with the services were coded as having a low particularized-referent need. Those whose answers indicated overall dissatisfaction were categorized as having high particularized need. Dran and Smith's analysis supported the hypothesis that need is primary in generating both types of contacts and that, for people at a given level of need of either type, individuals with higher SES are more likely to initiate a contact.

By way of summary, table 2-3 classifies each of the relevant studies of contacting in terms of its position on the crucial question of who contacts and why, specifically the SES-contacting relationship.

Race and Contacting

Two final parts of an answer to the question "Who contacts?" remain to be considered. One concerns the extent to which particularized contactors engage in other modes of political participation; it is discussed fully in chapter 4. The other concerns racial differences in propensity to contact. Is there racial disparity in contacting? Three answers to this question are possible: there is no difference in black and white contacting rates, blacks contact at higher rates, or whites contact at higher rates. In fact, available research suggests all three conclusions.

The large national survey conducted by Verba and Nie (1972) in the late 1960s found considerable racial difference in contact rates, with whites contacting more often. They discovered that, even when they adjusted the data for racial differences in income, occupation, and education, blacks still exhibited a significantly lower contact rate than whites. They concluded, "The disparity between black and white contacting behavior that remains after one has removed the effects of education, income, and occupational level clearly suggests that there is indeed some racial barrier to such activity, as there is to a lesser extent with voting" (Verba and Nie, 1972:162). Further analysis of their data indicated that blacks were much more likely than whites to feel that they could not directly contact an official but needed a "go-between" and that they were much more likely than whites to think they would have trouble finding such a go-between if they wanted one (Verba and Nie, 1972:165–67).

Sharp (1980) carried this line of research one step farther in her analysis of survey data from St. Louis, Missouri; Tampa, Florida; and Rochester, New York. She found that blacks were less likely than whites to have recognized an "advocacy contact" channel, even when controlling for political efficacy, and that blacks are more likely than whites to recognize a citizen organization as a contact channel.

Hero's (1986) analysis of a sample of adult residents of Colorado Springs, a city with a sizable Chicano population, showed only a very negligible simple relationship between minority racial/ethnic

Table 2-3. **Classification of Contact Studies by Relationship of SES to Contacting**

Study	SES-contacting relationship			
	Moderate or strong positive	Negligible or null	Downward-opening parabola	Strong negative
Eisinger (1972)	Milwaukee (survey)			
Shin and Everson (1980)	3 Illinois cities (survey)			
Vedlitz and Veblen (1980)	Garland, TX (survey)			
Brown (1982)	Kitchener, Can. (survey)			
Sharp (1982)	Wichita (survey)			
Steger, Vertz, and Wirth (1982)	U.S.A. central cities (survey)			
Thomas (1982)	Cincinnati (survey)			
Dran and Smith (1984)	Detroit (survey)			
Friedman (1974)		Alberta; Britain (survey)		

Jacob (1972)	Milwaukee (survey)
Hero (1986)	Colorado Springs (survey)
Verba and Nie (1972)	U.S.A. (survey)
Mladenka (1977)	Houston (aggregate)
Sharp (1984a)	Kansas city (survey)
Jones et al. (1977)	Detroit (aggregate)
Bachelor (1983)	Detroit (aggregate)
Vedlitz, Dyer, and Durand (1980)	Dallas; Houston (aggregate)
Burnett, Cole, and Moon (1983)	Portsmouth, England (aggregate)

Note: Type of data appears in parentheses.

status and contacting. However, when he controlled the influence of age, perceived need, and efficacy, ethnic/racial status revealed significant and sizable negative relationships with two out of three measures of contacting. Members of ethnic and racial minority groups in Colorado Springs are much less likely to contact than whites.

Data from Milwaukee support these negative conclusions. Both Jacob (1972) and Eisinger (1972) found that whites are much more likely to initiate a contact than blacks. Whites made opinion contacts more frequently than request contacts, but blacks made request contacts more often than opinion contacts. Bachelor (1983) found in Detroit that black neighborhoods generated more contacts alleging poor city services, while white neighborhoods produced more complaints against fellow citizens.

Several other studies, including both survey and aggregate data methods, found black "overparticipation" by means of contacting rather than a relatively low contact rate. Thomas (1982), in his research on Cincinnati, found that black residents initiated more contacts than whites about buildings and inspection complaints, even when need for city services was controlled. Jones et al. (1977) found that, in Detroit, neighborhoods with a higher proportion of black residents were more likely to initiate contacts about environmental enforcement complaints (e.g., litter, weeds, rats, and containers) when the influence of neighborhood social well-being was controlled. Shin and Everson (1980:23) found blacks slightly "overrepresented" among the contactors in all three Illinois cities they studied.

Most interestingly, Haeberle (1986) found that race had no impact on requests for city action in Birmingham, when the analysis controlled for SES, environmental conditions, and another participation variable. He measured race as predominantly black (a dummy variable for 85 percent or more black) and as racial homogeneity (the absolute value of the difference between the percentage of black and white residents in each neighborhood). Neither variable affected contacting. Similarly, in Dallas, Mladenka (1977) found no racial differences in contacts among ten content categories nor in contact rate.

It is difficult to determine generally whether blacks contact at higher or lower rates than whites when the effect of socioeconomic status is controlled. The evidence seems to indicate that black contact rates may be higher if particularized-referent contacts about neighborhood environmental quality are considered. Otherwise, it appears that whites contact at higher rates.

Who contacts, why, about what, and how often? Academic research addressing these questions provides a variety of answers. Why have different researchers produced different answers? Are the answers different because each city is unique? Or do answers differ because investigators used different (and fallible) research methods, even when cities tend to be alike?

Explaining the Contradictory Findings

Is it possible that all cities are unique and that citizen-initiated contacting in each is explained by an idiosyncratic combination of forces? In what relevant ways might cities differ greatly? Five potentially important differences are evident.

First, some municipalities have centralized complaint-handling agencies responsible for receiving and referring all citizen contacts, for monitoring activities of agencies to which contacts are referred, and for ensuring that bureaucratic agencies are responsive to citizen contacts. Existence of a centralized complaint center or "ombudsman" may be extensively advertised in a municipality, and advertisement constitutes information that produces awareness. If awareness becomes widely distributed throughout the city's spatial and socioeconomic groups, then awareness of government's responsibility, responsiveness, and telephone number is more equally distributed across all income and education groups. If awareness is more equally distributed, then need might become relatively more important, indeed perhaps the dominant influence. The relative importance of need and awareness may be a function of the existence (and advertisement) of a central complaint agency (Vedlitz, Dyer, and Durand, 1980:65–66).

Contacting Kansas City's Action Center, according to Sharp (1984a:97–120), showed a strong, significant, negative association with neighborhood social well-being. She argued that the correlation existed because awareness of the Action Center was relatively equally spread across neighborhoods. She found that other forms of political information, such as awareness of public officials, were not so evenly distributed.

Second, different cities may be dominated by different political subcultures, that is, by different basic values about the purpose of the political system. Some citizens feel that local government is designed to serve the public interest, the needs of the entire community, and the general welfare. They are more likely to initiate broad-referent contact with government. Other citizens feel that local government exists to serve the needs of particular subcommunities or groups within the city by distributing material favors or rewards rather than by exercising governmental power for programmatic ends. These people would more likely initiate particularistic contact (Banfield and Wilson, 1963; Eisinger, 1972:55; Elazar, 1984; Shin and Everson, 1980).

A third possible explanation for the divergence of findings about who contacts pertains to the variety of functional responsibilities undertaken by American local government. The fact that Garland, Texas, operates its own electric and water companies is probably responsible for many contacts about individual households' monthly bills, and these contacts are probably fairly equally distributed across most income groups. Complaints about utility rates differ from those about rodents and abandoned houses (Vedlitz and Veblen, 1980).

A fourth and possibly related reason for the different findings is the large socioeconomic differences among American cities. Declining cities with relatively old and dilapidated housing stock and substantial poverty might differ from relatively young, affluent, growing cities in the nature of contacts produced. The latter type of municipality could yield a negative linear relationship between social well-being and contacting rather than a parabolic relationship, because the social well-being variable is truncated at the low end. In such cities, if there were more poor people in more neighborhoods experiencing more negative environmental externalities, the curve might slope upward, level off, then slope downward, indicating highest contact rates among middle-income groups, as the Jones et al. need-awareness model stipulated (Vedlitz, Dyer, and Durand, 1980).

Finally, some municipalities have prominent black mayors and/
or department heads. Black citizens might contact at higher rates
when local government is made more salient to them through election of a black mayor. They might feel more comfortable and
efficacious complaining to a building and inspections department if
its chief official is black. Whites might contact less often in such a
situation.

The alternative to considering each city unique is to assume that
identical factors influence the propensity to contact in all cities and
that researchers' use of different methodologies is responsible for
their differences in findings. Four such reasons are evident. First,
the standard socioeconomic model might have produced various
results because it has been applied to (a) all contacts, (b) general-
referent contacts, and (c) particularized contacts. Perhaps it yields
different results when applied to different types of contacts because socioeconomically different people generate different rates
of contacts with different referents and contents.

A second reason relates to differences between the microanalytic approach using survey data and the macroanalytic approach using aggregate data. Researchers cannot safely generalize
the behavior of individuals to a neighborhood. Nor can the behavior of neighborhoods be generalized to individuals. Whites, for
example, might contact more when they live in relatively black
neighborhoods. Middle-income residents might complain more
when they live in relatively poor neighborhoods (Jones et al., 1977).
No researcher has collected both micro and macro data in a single
municipality at a single point in time to try to resolve this methodological problem.

Third, key concepts were measured differently by different researchers. Contacting in an aggregate data study might be measured as number of calls to a centralized complaint agency per
1,000 population in each census tract. Or contacting might be measured in a survey as a response to a question, "Have you ever
contacted . . . ?" The variety of ways to ask this question in a
survey was discussed earlier. Similarly, socioeconomic status and
the need for government service can be measured in quite different
ways. Some studies measured "objective need" (Bachelor, 1983;
Jones et al., 1977)—that is, they used aggregate census data to
describe community or neighborhood problems. Survey re-

searchers used measures of "perceived need" (e.g., Dran and Smith, 1984:11; Sharp, 1984a:44)—that is, the extent to which survey respondents feel there are problems in their neighborhood for which government is responsible.

Use of different measures of statistical association might provide a fourth, related reason for such a diversity of conclusions. Some investigators used Pearson's coefficient of correlation to measure the extent to which SES and contacting are related. Pearson's coefficient measures linear association only, even when curvilinear association is present. Other researchers used gamma, which measures linear relationships but is also sensitive to curvilinearity. Gamma coefficients might actually have provided evidence in support of the parabolic need-awareness model, while the investigator assumed that it provided confirmation of the linear socioeconomic model.

Finally, the problem might lie in misspecification of the explanatory equation—in other words, one or more key explanatory variables might have been missing from most investigators' research. For example, there is reason to suspect that citizen-initiated contacting might be strongly influenced by political mobilization at the neighborhood level (Haeberle, 1986; Sharp, 1984a:51–97). Cities with several strong neighborhood associations might experience their highest contact rates from the areas where these associations operate. Those neighborhoods might be relatively poor, or they could be middle class, as Rich (1979; 1980) suggested. Perhaps if strength of neighborhood political mobilization were included in explanations, American cities would exhibit a more uniform pattern of relationship between socioeconomic status and contacting.

The next chapter examines some of these questions in detail with respect to contacting in Birmingham, Alabama. It is especially concerned to determine who contacts the Birmingham Mayor's Office of Citizens Assistance, why, about what, and with what effect. The main purpose is to identify a model that best explains patterns of contacting in Birmingham.

3

Testing the Models:

Contacting in Birmingham, Alabama

The main purpose of this chapter is to examine empirically several of the models relating SES and contacting that were presented in chapter 2. Contact data collected in 1983 for Birmingham, Alabama, a city of approximately 300,000 population, are used in multiple regression analysis to test the models hypothesizing null or negligible, moderate or strong, positive, negative, or curvilinear relationships between SES and contacting. The effect of race on contacting is also examined. As we shall see, the pattern of contacting in Birmingham fits none of the previous models, and a new one will be constructed.

A second purpose of this chapter is to describe the effect of contact experience on the contactors. A random sample survey of contactors provides the data necessary to measure citizens' satisfaction with their experience. Thus both aggregate and survey data are analyzed in this chapter.

The Mayor's Office of Citizens Assistance serves as Birmingham's centralized complaint center. A 50 percent sample of citizen contacts received during 1983 was examined for content of contact, agency to which the complaint was referred, distribution of contacts across months of the year, and distribution of contacts across areas of the city. This chapter presents an analysis of evidence collected from MOCA archives.

The Content of Contacts

The year 1983 may or may not be typical with respect to the volume, type, and distribution of calls received by MOCA. One

39

Table 3-1. Content of MOCA Contacts

Category	N	Percentage
Overgrowth	562	34
Trash, refuse	374	23
Streets and sidewalks	288	17
Buildings and housing	190	11
Sewage, drainage	90	6
Animal control	68	4
Other	78	5
Total	1,650	100

year is long enough, however, to give at least a strong indication of representative patterns of contacting. Table 3-1 presents distribution of contacts by content. It is immediately evident that virtually all the contacts are particularized. A huge majority of the contactors called to complain about some problem in the immediate vicinity of their own residences.

Over one-third of all contacts constitute complaints about overgrowth of vacant lots, with the attendant problems of neighborhood aesthetics and public safety. Complaints about refuse, trash, debris, and abandoned vehicles comprise almost 23 percent of all calls. Another large category, about 17 percent of all contacts, is complaints about streets and sidewalks, including potholes, missing or needed street lights and signs, and other inconvenient or dangerous conditions. The only other sizable category, buildings and housing, produced over 11 percent of all complaints. It concerns building code violations, abandoned buildings, landlord-tenant disputes, and so forth. The top three categories—overgrowth, trash and refuse, and streets—comprise almost three-quarters of all contacts. These three categories are predominantly concerned with particularized contacts about environmental beauty and safety in the contactors' neighborhoods. They pertain to basic municipal services of a physical and environmental nature.

MOCA refers its contacts to over ten municipal departments for action. As table 3-2 indicates, however, approximately two-thirds of all complaints are referred to a single agency, the Street and

Table 3-2. **Municipal Departments to Which MOCA Refers Contacts**

Departments	N	Percentage
Street and Sanitation	1,090	66
Building and Inspection Services	214	13
Traffic Engineering	124	8
Engineering	92	6
Health	70	4
Community Development	12	1
Other	50	3
Total	1,652	100

Sanitation Department. The Department of Building and Inspection Services handles the second highest number of referred complaints, at 13 percent of the total. Without good estimates of the number of direct citizen contacts with each of these ten agencies, it is impossible to draw final conclusions about all citizen complaints in Birmingham. It is possible that citizens consider MOCA primarily a contact agency for problems of the sort handled by the Street and Sanitation Department and generally call agencies concerned with other types of problems directly. In any case, the connection between MOCA and the Street and Sanitation Department is clearly the most important one.

Seasonal Distribution

Distribution of MOCA contacts across time is also informative. Seasonal distribution is important to municipal decision makers because it indicates optimal personnel distribution patterns. Additional, perhaps temporary part-time personnel can be hired to respond to requests during particularly high-demand months. Similarly, employees might be shifted from one municipal department to another in periods when the former has fewer demands and the latter more.

Table 3-3 presents both the number and percentage of all contacts by months of the year. Clearly the summer months of June

Table 3-3. **Monthly Distribution of MOCA Contacts**

Month	All MOCA contacts		MOCA contacts referred to Street and Sanitation Department	
	Number	Percentage	Number	Percentage
January	62	3.6	31	50
February	61	3.6	35	57
March	93	5.5	52	56
April	88	5.2	62	70
May	135	8.0	97	72
June	245	14.4	214	87
July	234	13.8	179	77
August	188	11.1	151	80
September	209	12.3	177	85
October	194	11.4	144	74
November	57	3.4	41	72
December	128	7.5	92	77
Total	1,694	100.0	1,275	—

through October comprise the period of greatest activity. These five months comprise 42 percent of the year in time but contain over 63 percent of the requests for service. June and July are the two peak months. January and February are the least active months, with only 3.6 percent of the contacts each. May can be considered a "normal" month with 8 percent of the volume, since 8.3 percent is $1/12$, or an equal monthly share. November, December, and January through April are relatively low-volume periods.

Since contacts referred to the Street and Sanitation Department are such a large proportion of all calls, table 3-3 also contains a monthly tabulation of those calls. It is evident that the large volume of MOCA summer contacts is strongly influenced by increased reporting of problems normally referred to Street and Sanitation. During the five summer months, Street and Sanitation referrals comprise fully 80 percent of the total volume of MOCA's complaints. During the other seven months of the year, Street and Sanitation referrals average only 65 percent of the total calls. They are close to half during January through March.

During 1983, MOCA served primarily as an answering service for the large number of citizen complaints about problems normally dealt with by the Street and Sanitation Department. This pattern of interaction makes the relationship between MOCA and the Street and Sanitation Department especially important in responding to the requests of Birmingham residents.

Spatial Distribution

Analysis of the spatial distribution of MOCA contacts indicates the geographical sources of complaints within the City of Birmingham. As figure 3-1 indicates, some areas produce virtually no complaints and other areas generate a relatively heavy concentration of contacts. Figure 3-1 presents pure volume of contacts of all kinds. The darkest areas represent the highest volume of demand for MOCA and bureaucratic agency services. The less dark areas represent sections of Birmingham with considerable demand for service, while the light gray areas produced still fewer contacts. The solid white areas generated a very low volume of contacts.

This depiction of the spatial distribution of pure volume of contacts in all likelihood reflects both the population size of each census tract and any "causal" forces such as need and civic attitudes. Generally, areas with a larger population, especially where there is greater population density, would be expected to produce more contacts—more people, therefore more contacts.

If one combines the two solid dark areas that indicate at least 11 contacts per census tract in figure 3-1, there is a prominent inverted U or horseshoe-shaped distribution of high-volume contact tracts in central Birmingham. Some exceptions are indicated by light gray and white tracts, but basically demand assumes the shape of a horseshoe around the central business district. To this area city personnel must travel most often to perform inspections, repairs, construction, condemnations, mowing, clean-ups, explanations, and so forth.

Absence of complaints is just as noticeable in the northern tier of tracts. These areas produce few or no complaints to MOCA, and consequently city personnel make relatively few visits to these areas to respond to specific requests.

Figure 3-1. The Spatial Distribution of MOCA Contacts among Census Tracts in Birmingham, Alabama

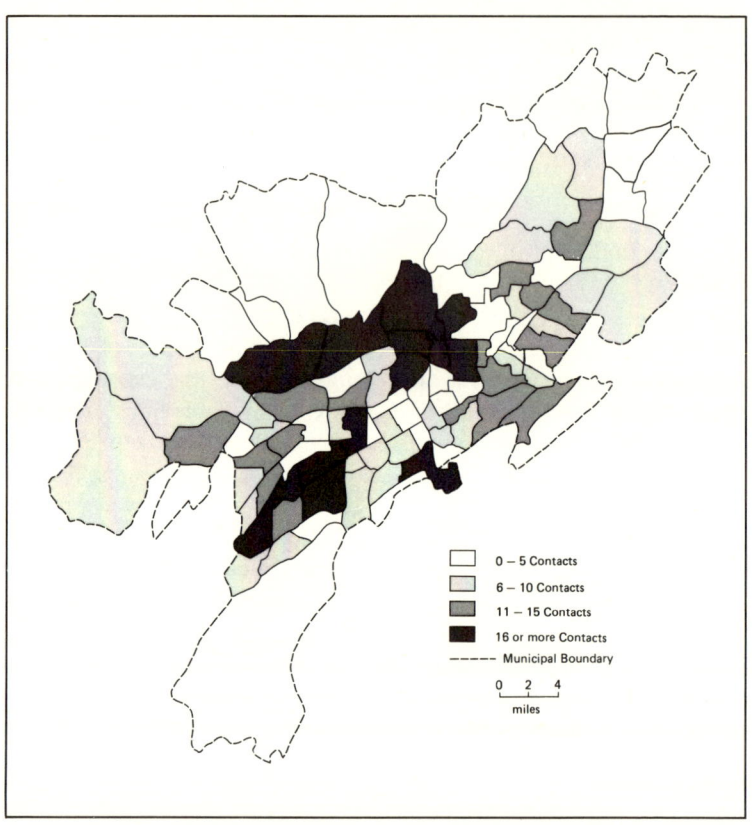

```
      □   0 – 5 Contacts
      ▨   6 – 10 Contacts
      ▨   11 – 15 Contacts
      ■   16 or more Contacts
      ----- Municipal Boundary

          0   2   4
          └───┴───┘
             miles
```

Figure 3-2 maps the spatial distribution of contacts among census tracts while controlling for tract population size, that is, contacts per 1,000 population. Variations in the map are therefore more likely to reflect distribution of "causal" forces in each census tract rather than population size. Figure 3-2 presents several interesting contrasts with the map in figure 3-1. Contacts per 1,000 population do not present as clear a pattern as simple volume of contacts. The darkest tracts, representing highest demand per capita, appear in all areas of the city. Per capita demand for MOCA services cer-

Figure 3-2. The Spatial Distribution of MOCA Contacts per 1,000 Population among Census Tracts in Birmingham, Alabama

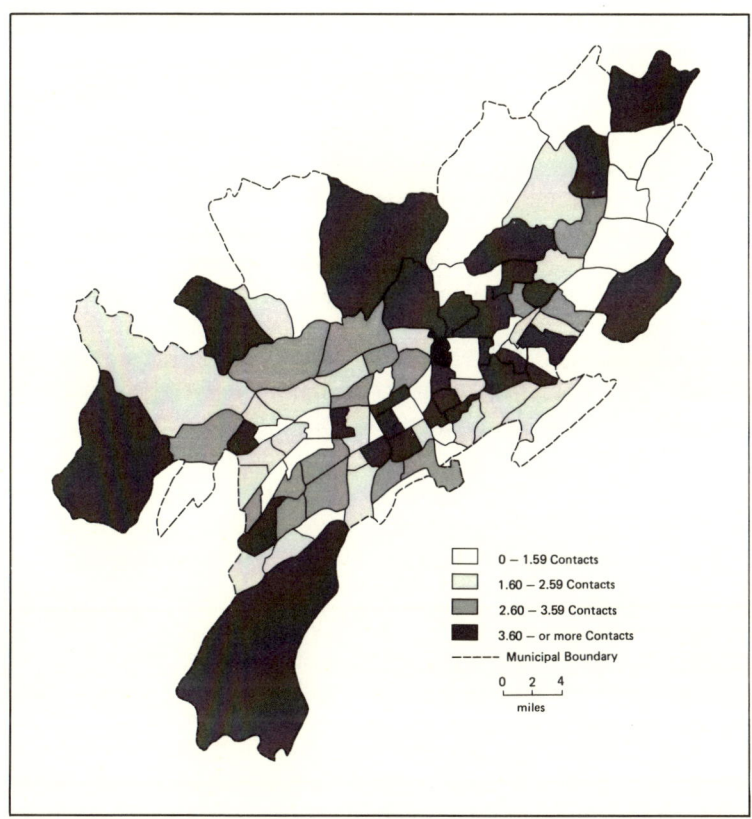

0 – 1.59 Contacts
1.60 – 2.59 Contacts
2.60 – 3.59 Contacts
3.60 – or more Contacts
----- Municipal Boundary

0   2   4
miles

tainly does not form the previously seen horseshoe around the central business district. And the northern tier of tracts includes both lowest and highest demand per capita areas. There are several lowest-demand tracts in the inner city and several in the suburban periphery.

When population size of tract is controlled, as in figure 3-2, contact propensity appears to be geographically unpatterned. Presumably the standard socioeconomic model, a need model, or the need-awareness model can explain this spatially unpatterned distribution of contacts.

Who Contacts? Socioeconomic Status, Need, and Race

The 828 MOCA contacts sampled were geocoded to 96 census tracts, which are the unit of analysis. Only 87 tracts could be used, however, because some were so small in population size that the U.S. Census Bureau suppressed socioeconomic and racial data to protect confidentiality. Census statistics characterizing the tracts can be correlated with contact frequency. Median family income of census tracts was chosen as the measure of general socioeconomic status or social well-being in Birmingham. The average income for all 87 census tracts was $14,944. The number of contacts from each tract was adjusted for tract population size, so that number of contacts does not reflect number of people. The average number of contacts per 1,000 population was 4.6.

TESTING THE STANDARD SES, NULL, AND NEED MODELS

Pearson's product-moment correlation coefficient between contacts and median family income in Birmingham was very small, negative, and nonsignificant ($-.08$). In other words, the standard socioeconomic model totally fails to account for propensity to contact in Birmingham. There is simply no positive linear relationship between socioeconomic status and propensity to contact. Similarly, although the correlation coefficient is negative, it is too small to suggest that need for government services explains contacting in Birmingham. On the basis of the univariate analysis, it appears that the null model is most appropriate. Only multivariate analysis can indicate which model is most appropriate, however, and that analysis is presented later.

RACE AND CONTACTING

What about the relationship between race and propensity to contact MOCA? Do black citizens tend to contact more, less, or about as much as white residents? The simple correlation coefficient between contacting and percentage black for census tracts is a statistically significant − .14. This figure indicates that census tracts with a larger percentage of black residents tend to generate fewer contacts. However, the correlation coefficient between percentage black and median family income of census tracts is − .58, a strong and significant relationship. Census tracts with larger proportions of black residents tend to have substantially lower median family incomes. For this reason, the relationship between black percentage and contacting may be spurious, that is, it may be the low income of black residents, and not their race, that inhibits their contacting. The relationship between race and contacting is further explored later.

Testing the Need-Awareness Model

One way to test the Jones et al. model of a parabolic relationship between SES and contacting is multiple regression analysis. This form of analysis seeks to explain variations in contact rates among census tracts as a function of two variables—median family income and median family income squared. If there is a curvilinear relationship between contacting and SES, with middle-income areas exhibiting the highest contact rates, as Jones et al. (1977) found, then in the regression equation, the median family income coefficient will have a significant positive sign and the median family income-squared coefficient will have a negative sign. Such relationships indicate that, as one moves from low to middle SES, contacts increase. At the middle SES level, contacts are then at their highest point. As one moves from middle to high SES, contact rates decline. This model can be used to try to explain contacting in Birmingham.

The statistical equation used is a quadratic function:

$$C = a + b_1X_1 + b_2X_1^2,$$

where

C = contact rate across census tracts (adjusted for population size)

a = contact rate when income is 0$

b_1 = regression coefficient measuring the relative influence of median family income on contacting

X_1 = median family income

b_2 = regression coefficient measuring the relative influence of median family income squared on contacting

X_1^2 = median family income squared.

The objective is to estimate the extent to which contact rates are influenced by need and awareness. Recall the Jones et al. assumptions that need for government services is negatively associated with income and that awareness is positively associated with income. Estimating the parabolic equation using data from MOCA contacts produces the equation in table 3-4.

Table 3-4. **Regression of Contacting on Income**

	Regression coefficient	Statistical significance
Income	−.0023	.0005
Income-squared	+.000000064	.0005
Constant	21.2	
$R = .49$	$R^2 = .24$	$p = .01$

The results presented in table 3-4 are the opposite of that found by Jones et al. Contacting exhibits a strong curvilinear relationship with income, but the lowest contact rates are found among the middle-income tracts and the highest rates are found in the lowest- and highest-income tracts. The sign attached to income is negative; the sign attached to income squared is positive. Both are extremely significant; their F-values indicate that there are only 5 chances in 10,000 that these results are due to random variance. Figure 3-3 presents a graph of the curve describing this relationship, a U-shaped, upward-opening parabola. Fully 24 percent of the variance in propensity to contact is statistically explained by this fitted curve ($R = .49$, $R^2 = .24$).

Figure 3-3. The Relationship between SES and MOCA Contacts

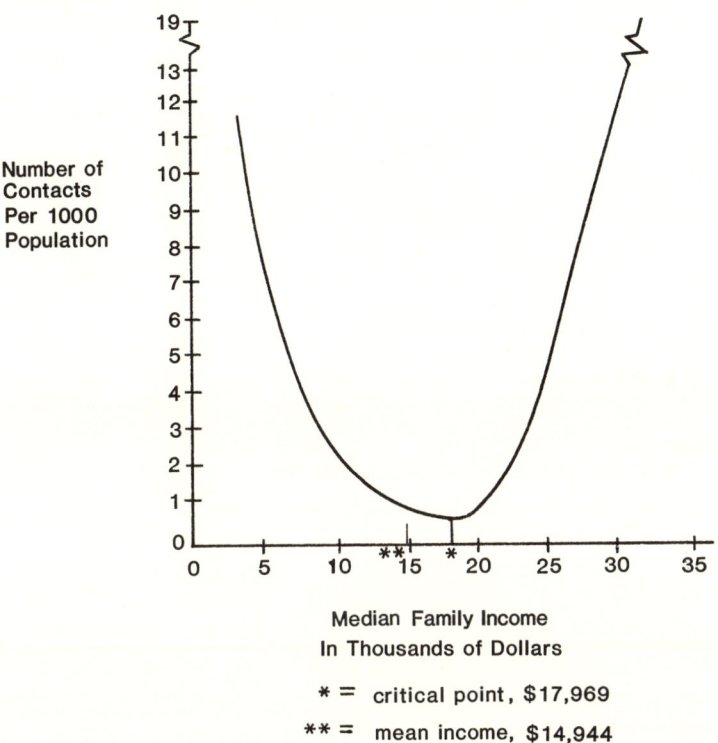

Median Family Income
In Thousands of Dollars

* = critical point, $17,969

** = mean income, $14,944

The results of this analysis indicate that the darkest areas in figure 3-2 are census tracts with relatively low and high median family income. The white areas are those tracts with roughly middle-income residents. Obviously the distribution says something about the conventionally hypothesized relationship between SES and both need and awareness: it is not operative in Birmingham. Something causes low- and high-income neighborhoods to generate a relatively high number of contacts. In terms of the need-awareness model, it appears that residents of areas with substantial need (low income) overcome their negative civic attitudes and contact MOCA relatively frequently. Residents of areas with strongly positive civic attitudes (high income) apparently feel significant need, because they also contact relatively frequently.

Basic differential calculus procedure can be used to determine the point on the income scale where the slope of the curve changes from negative to positive, that is, where increases in income stop producing decreases in contacting and start producing increases. The procedure involves computing the first derivative of Y for the quadratic function specified earlier, equating the derivative to zero, and solving for X_1. In this case, the value of X_1 will indicate the median family income level at which the contact rate is lowest.

The derivative of Y is expressed as $X^* = dy/dx = -.0023 + .000000128X_1$. This quantity is the slope of the function when the derivative equals zero. If the derivative equation is set equal to zero and is solved for X_1, $X^* = \$17,969$, called the critical point. Birmingham's per capita contact rate is at its lowest in tracts with a median family income of $17,969. Income and contacting are negatively associated in tracts with median family income lower than this critical point. Income and contacting are positively related in tracts with income higher than $17,969. Figure 3-3 illustrates the value of the derivative in the curve describing the income-contact relationship in Birmingham.

Computation of the critical value, $17,969, permits further interpretation of the parabolic regression equation and figure 3-3. First, only sixteen tracts have incomes above the critical point; the other seventy tracts have incomes below that figure. Seventy cases are responsible for the negative slope of the curve, and only sixteen cases are responsible for the positive upturn. If low income represents greater need for government services, a reasonable assumption, clearly need dominates the curve in figure 3-3. It should also be noticed that the critical income at which the slope of the curve changes from negative to positive is $3,025 greater than the mean income for all eighty-seven tracts, as also indicated in figure 3-3.

A second point of interpretation concerns the slope of the negative and positive areas of the curve. The slope of the curve, or the instantaneous rate of change in contacting produced by a marginal change in income, can be computed at any tract income level, and in a curvilinear function it will differ at different values of the independent variable. Table 3-5 presents the instantaneous rate of

Table 3-5. **Rates of Change in Contacting Produced by Marginal Increases in Income**

Income level $(X_i)(\$)$	Rate of change in contacting (dy/dx)
5,000	− 0.00166
7,000	− 0.00140
14,000	− 0.00051
16,000	− 0.00025
17,969[a]	0.00000[a]
28,000	0.00128
30,000	0.00154
32,000	0.00181

[a] = Critical point.

change in contacting *(dy)* produced by a marginal increase in income *(dx)* at eight representative levels of income (X_i).

Table 3-5 indicates that the parabolic curve describing the relationship between income and contacting is approximately symmetrical. A marginal change in income at the highest income levels produces approximately the same rate of change in contacting that is produced by a marginal change in income at the lowest income levels. For example, the $2,000 increase from $5,000 to $7,000 produces an 18.5 percent change in the rate of decline, or slope. An identical $2,000 increase from $28,000 to $30,000 results in a 20 percent change in the rate of increase.

The equation in table 3-6 includes percentage black residents as a third explanatory variable. Birmingham's eighty-seven usable census tracts averaged 52.9 percent black in the 1980 census. The purpose of this equation is to determine whether areas with a higher proportion of black residents contact more or less frequently when the effect of income on contacting is controlled. In other words, if all census tracts in Birmingham had the same median family income, would tracts with more black residents contact less than, as much as, or more than tracts with a lower percentage of black residents?

Areas with higher proportions of black residents contact at lower rates even when the influence of income on contacting is controlled. The sign of the percentage black variable is negative.

Table 3-6. **Regression of Contacting on Income and Race**

		Regression coefficient	Statistical significance
Income		−.0024	.0001
Income-squared		+.000000062	.0005
Percent black		−.066	.01
Constant		27.3	
	$R = .54$	$R^2 = .29$	$p = .01$

There could be many reasons, but two come immediately to mind: actual discrimination and the perception by blacks that contacting city government will do no good. The income variable again has an extremely significant negative coefficient, and the income-squared variable again has an extremely significant positive coefficient. The percentage black coefficient is also significant at an acceptable level ($p = .01$). If percentage black increases by twenty-five percentage points, propensity to contact is likely to decrease by 1.6 contacts per 1,000 population, in the average census tract, when the income effect is controlled. Adding percentage black to the equation explains an additional five percentage points of variance in contacting beyond that explained in table 3-4; $R = .54, R^2 = .29$.

A summary of findings from tables 3-4 and 3-6 to this point is in order. The median family income variable indexes individual households' incomes in each census tract. As income increases from the poorest ($4,609) to approximately $17,969, contact rate decreases. At $17,969, contact rate is at its lowest. As family income increases from $17,969 up to the income of the wealthiest families ($34,000), contact rate increases. In other words, tracts with the poorest and the wealthiest median family income contact the most. But even if all families had the same income, tracts with greater proportions of black residents would still contact at a significantly lower rate than tracts with lower proportions of black residents.

Another variable, median value of owner-occupied housing, is now added to form a third equation. This variable, which averaged

$31,467 among Birmingham's eighty-seven census tracts, is used to measure the quality or strength of homeowners' long-term financial and personal investment in their neighborhoods. It measures *financial* investment because it indexes the estimated dollar value of the investment that residents have made for housing in a given neighborhood. It represents *personal* investment because it refers only to residents who live in the homes in which they have invested, in their neighborhoods. Homeowners tend to live in their neighborhoods longer than do renters, and this difference also indicates homeowners' personal stake in their neighborhoods. It distinguishes them as a group from persons who own housing but do not live in it, such as absentee landlords who have a financial investment but not the personal investment. Housing value measures the value of property and housing owned and lived in by a *subset* of tract residents. As such, it probably represents the physical and environmental conditions of a tract rather than the income of tract residents. Many middle- and even some upper-income families rent the housing in which they live, and families of varying income levels live in single-family homes of similar market value. Thus the housing value variable measures neighborhood property values rather than residential income.

Sharp (1984b:68–70) argued for homeownership as an index of "stakeholding" in a neighborhood but did not find that homeowners are more prone to perceive "big problems" in their neighborhoods than are others. In fact, in the neighborhoods that were best off by objective standards, homeowners were significantly less likely to perceive big problems in their immediate vicinity. However, adding owner-occupied housing value to table 3-6 represents a possible improvement in measurement for two reasons. First, it controls for the effects of race and especially income, thereby avoiding identification of a possibly spurious relationship between homeowning and contacting. Second, it includes *value* of the home owned, not just *whether* a home is owned.

The dollar value of the home in which residents both invest and live represents their degree of incentive to protect their long-term financial and personal investment. Median family income probably disproportionately measures lower-income residents' need for government services to correct basic physical and environmental deterioration in their neighborhoods, whereas owner-occupied housing value more likely measures the incentive of homeowners to protect existing property values and life-style in their neighborhoods. Presumably, the greater the value, the stronger the incentive to protect it. The impetus to contact presumably becomes even stronger when local problems impinge on the homeowner by threatening to devalue the investment (Thomas, 1985). Leaving the neighborhood (Hirschman, 1970) is not an attractive option even to a household facing problems because of "transaction costs," such as selling one home, finding another, buying another, moving the family and belongings, and so forth (Cox, 1982). Therefore, it is hypothesized that the variable—value of owner-occupied housing—will have a positive linear relationship with contacting when income and race are controlled.

Neither income nor housing value seems to measure awareness in the equation in table 3-7, but awareness is probably not an important influence on contacting in the context of strong need to correct neighborhood deterioration or strong incentive to preserve neighborhood property values and amenities. Residents with either sufficient need or sufficient incentive would probably acquire the psychological capacity to initiate a contact, and nothing more is required.

Including housing value produces table 3-7.

Table 3-7. **Regression of Contacting on Income, Race, and Owner-occupied Housing Value**

	Regression coefficient	*Statistical significance*
Income	−.0024	.0001
Income-squared	+.000000038	.01
Percent black	−.055	.01
Owner-occupied housing value	+.00043	.01
Constant	18.8	
$R = .60$ $R^2 = .36$ $p = .01$		

The Pearson's simple correlation coefficient between average owner-occupied housing value and contacting is a significant .16. It has a positive, statistically significant coefficient in table 3-7. When the effects of income and race are controlled, increases in owner-occupied housing value produce significant increases in contacting. This finding suggests that, if the income and racial composition of all of Birmingham's census tracts were identical, tracts with more high-value owner-occupied houses would generate more contacts. Residents of more valuable owner-occupied housing seem to have a greater stake in their neighborhoods and contact city government more frequently to request services. The equation in table 3-7 explains seven percentage points more variance in contact behavior than the previous equation, with only income and race (R = .60, R^2 = .36).

Not only is housing value significant and positive when added to the equation, but interesting changes occur in the other explanatory variables already in the equation. Income, income squared, and race all remain statistically significant, even though there is some collinearity between pairs of them. More important, the addition of housing value increases the size and significance of the income coefficient and reduces the importance of the income-squared coefficient.

Figure 3-4 presents for comparison the curves fitted by the income equation and the full equation containing income, race, and median value of owner-occupied housing. The R^2 indicates that the curve produced by the full equation has superior goodness of fit with the data. Differences in the shapes of the two curves graphically indicate where, along the income scale, adding housing value and race helps to explain contact rates further. The two additional variables provide more explanatory power from the poorest families to those with median incomes of about $15,000. Even more explanation of contacting is added in the $15,000 to $18,000 range. The curves are contiguous for tracts with income between $20,000 and $25,000, indicating that the full equation predicts no better than the income equation for that income range. However, the curves diverge considerably for tracts with income above $25,000, the area of greatest improvement produced by adding race and housing value.

Figure 3-4. Contact Curves Estimated by Income Equation and Full Equation

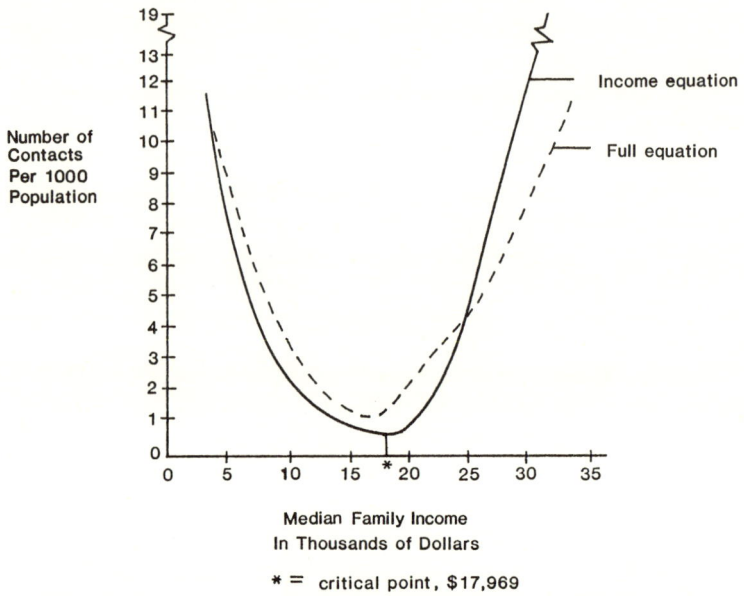

Median Family Income
In Thousands of Dollars

* = critical point, $17,969

Contacts with MOCA in Birmingham clearly do not conform to any of the prominent models found in the literature, although they approximate a need model in certain important ways. Further discussion of why the major models fail to account for contacting in Birmingham and further explanation of the results produced by the full equation appear in chapter 5. In the meantime let us consider contactors' reactions to their contact experience, particularly in terms of their satisfaction with MOCA.

Client Satisfaction with MOCA

It is important to determine the effect on citizens of MOCA's responses to their contacts. In order to assess the level of citizen satisfaction with MOCA performance, a systematic random sample of 279 MOCA contactors from January through June 1984 was interviewed by the Capstone Poll. Respondents were asked a variety of questions about their experience as MOCA contactors.

Table 3-8. **Contactors' Sources of Information about MOCA**

Sources of information	Percentage
1. Mayor's office	22
2. Neighbor, friend, family member	19
3. Neighborhood association meeting	16
4. Government office	13
5. City hall telephone operator	9
6. Telephone book	9
7. Newspaper and/or television	7
8. Other	5
Total	100

Question: How did you first find out about the Office of Citizens Assistance?

As a relatively new organization, MOCA has an interest in establishing its name and function as a centralized complaint unit throughout the city. One question in the survey was designed to identify contactors' sources of information about the existence of MOCA. Table 3-8 presents the results. Over one-fifth (22 percent) of all contactors learned of MOCA by first calling the mayor's office and being told to call MOCA. An almost equal number, 19 percent, learned about MOCA through more informal word-of-mouth means, for example, from friends, neighbors, and family members. Neighborhood association meetings provided information about MOCA to another 16 percent of all respondents. A sizable number of contactors first contacted "city hall" (13 percent) or an official in some other government agency (9 percent) and were informed of MOCA's existence. About 9 percent of the contactors simply looked in a telephone directory and found the name and number of MOCA as an appropriate agency to call in order to register a complaint or request. Finally, only 7 percent of the contactors discovered MOCA's existence through the media, that is, through newspapers and television.

Another question in the survey was designed to measure contactors' assessment of the courteousness of MOCA personnel in handling their contact. Results of that question are contained in table 3-9. Contactors are virtually unanimous in evaluating MOCA

Table 3-9. Contactors' Evaluation of MOCA's
Courteousness

Response	Percentage
Yes	96
No	4
Total	100

Question: When you called, was the person you spoke to at the Office of Citizens Assistance courteous?

personnel as courteous. This level of agreement is extremely rare and unlikely unless MOCA personnel are, indeed, constantly courteous.

When a citizen calls to register a complaint or to make a request, especially with respect to some problem with a personal, particularized referent, he/she rightly wants to know how and when city government is going to deal with the complaint or request. It is important, therefore, for an office such as MOCA to provide each contactor with such information. Table 3-10 contains contactors' evaluation of MOCA's provision of information about how the city would handle the problem. MOCA's ability to communicate this information clearly is important to its success. Approximately two-thirds of the MOCA clients sampled indicated that they had been provided with an adequate amount of information.

Response time is a key feature of any public service to citizens. Even good service delivered too slowly is often viewed by the

Table 3-10. Contactors' Evaluation of MOCA's
Provision of Information

Response	Percentage
Yes	64
No	36
Total	100

Question: Did the person you talked with give you an adequate amount of information about how the city would handle your problem?

citizen as inadequate. Like the concept of "justice delayed is justice denied," even good service delayed may be service unappreciated. The survey asked all respondents about their perception of MOCA's response time. The data in table 3-11 indicate that about seven out of ten contactors felt that MOCA had responded in a reasonable period of time—that is, they were satisfied with the timeliness of MOCA's response to their requests.

Table 3-11. Contactors' Evaluation of MOCA's Response Time

Response	Percentage
Yes	70
No	30
Total	100

Question: Did the Office of Citizens Assistance handle your request for assistance within a reasonable length of time?

Respondents' answers to two other similar questions support their assessment of MOCA response as timely. They were asked whether they thought that some other city department might have handled their request faster than MOCA. Table 3-12 shows that an overwhelming majority, over 84 percent, expressed confidence that MOCA's response was faster than that of some other city government agency. Similarly, table 3-13 presents data on contactors' views about MOCA's value to a citizen who wants to initiate a

Table 3-12. Contactors' Comparative Evaluation of MOCA's Response Time

Response	Percentage
Yes	15
No	85
Total	100

Question: Do you think that your request might have been handled faster if you had called another city department instead of the Office of Citizens Assistance?

Table 3-13. Contactors' Evaluation of MOCA's
Facilitation of Citizen-Initiated Contact

Response	Percentage
Yes	89
No	11
Total	100

Question: Does having the Office of Citizens Assistance make it easier for people to request help from the city government?

contact with city government. Almost nine out of ten respondents agreed that MOCA's existence makes it easier for people to request help from the city.

One final evaluative question seeks to reveal the contactors' overall judgment of MOCA's effectiveness in handling requests. Answers to this question are more likely to reflect respondents' feelings about how well their problem was actually resolved by the relevant city government department, for example, Street and Sanitation or Traffic Engineering, than MOCA's operation as a central complaint-handling agency that refers requests to line departments. In any case, almost 90 percent of all respondents indicated that MOCA was positively helpful to them in seeing that their request was satisfied.

In summary, the results of this survey of MOCA clients suggest considerable success in dealing with citizen-initiated contacts. Large majorities of MOCA clients indicated that, when they initiated the contact, MOCA personnel were courteous, kept them properly informed, responded to their requests quickly and faster than alternative city agencies, and made contacting city government with a request easier than it would have been without MOCA. Citizen satisfaction with MOCA was high.

In order to establish an even clearer understanding of the extent to which citizens are aware of MOCA's existence and operation, presidents of Birmingham's ninety-three neighborhood associations were surveyed. A total of seventy-two presidents were interviewed. These neighborhood association officers are citizen-leaders whose responsibility includes working with their neigh-

Table 3-14. **Neighborhood Presidents' Identification of MOCA Director**

Response	Percentage
Correct[a]	30
Incorrect or	
don't know	70
Total	100

Note: N = 72.
[a]Answers such as "She works in the mayor's office" were accepted as correct.

borhoods' residents to improve the quality of their municipal public services. In this leadership role, they presumably serve as intermediaries between residents with a service complaint and city government as well as attempt to make residents aware of city government's service responsibilities. Tables 3-14 and 3-15 present results from two questions that bear upon MOCA's reputation among neighborhood citizen-leaders.

Less than one-third of the neighborhood leaders knew MOCA's director when they were told her name and were asked who she was. It might reasonably be expected that her name and title would be quite familiar to these leaders, whose responsibility for handling citizens' service complaints is considerable. Answers to the second question provide a partial explanation for their lack of knowledge. Neighborhood associations met twelve to sixteen times

Table 3-15. **Discussion of MOCA at Neighborhood Association Meetings**

Response	Percentage
Yes	53
No	47
Total	100

Question: At neighborhood meetings during the past two years, did you ever discuss the Mayor's Office of Citizens Assistance?
Note: N = 72.

during 1983. Only a little more than half of the presidents indicated that MOCA had ever been discussed at a neighborhood meeting during the past two years. Neighborhood presidents' answers to the two questions suggest that neither MOCA as a service complaint-and-request agency nor the name of its director was widely known among an extremely important stratum of citizen-activists in Birmingham.

Birmingham's contactors are clearly satisfied with both the process and results of their contacts. Let us now consider contactor characteristics, specifically contactors' political behavior beyond contacting.

4
Birmingham's Particularized Contactors:

Isolated Parochials or Complete Activists?

The review of recent citizen-initiated contact research in chapter 2 indicates that there is a basic consensus about the importance and virtual uniqueness of particularized contact with local government officials. Most of the literature also characterizes particularized contactors as isolated, parochial individuals who engage in few or no other forms of political participation. In fact, contactors are sometimes implicitly presented as self-centered and insatiable consumers of public goods who singlemindedly pursue immediate self-interest and have no conception of the broader political system or public interest. To what extent do Birmingham's particularized contactors engage in other forms of political participation?

To answer this question, we analyze data from three Birmingham surveys, two of the mass public and one of particularized contactors. Comparative analysis of these two populations permits us to draw some fairly firm conclusions about whether contactors are parochials or activists.

Conflicting Conclusions in the Literature

Verba and Nie, in their enormously influential *Participation in America,* stated: "Contacting on a narrow personal issue stands at one extreme of that dimension [scope of conflict], and it has no relationship to general political activity" (1972:67). In fact, they argued that "the unique position of particularized contacting suggests that we have found a mode of political activity that is not 'political' in the ordinary sense of the word" (Verba and Nie, 1972:71). In their factor analysis, particularized contacting loaded on a separate factor from campaign activity, voting, and cooperative activity/social contacting, and its Pearson product-moment correlation coefficients with these other participatory modes ranged from .06 to .10. Contacting had only a .15 correlation with their overall index of participation (Verba and Nie, 1972:75). Verba and Nie concluded that "the characteristics of particularized contacting suggest that we should find a group [of citizens] whose activity is limited to this mode of participation" (Verba and Nie, 1972:80). Their cluster analysis indicated that particularized contactors "engage in neither communal nor campaign activity, and are about average as voters" (ibid.). Finally, they argued that contacting is important mainly because it involves persons who might not otherwise participate or be heard from in expressing opinions and making demands upon the political system. Verba and Nie's work established the model with respect to conceptions of the contactor's political profile.

Vedlitz and Veblen (1980:34), in their study of Garland, Texas, also argued that contactors are isolated parochials: "Nearly half of the high voting participants report having no direct governmental contacts, while a similar fraction of contactors report low or medium voting activity." They found a gamma coefficient of association of only .31 between contacting and voting and concluded that "contacting seems to be an activity behaviorally independent of voting" (Vedlitz and Veblen, 1980:45). Furthermore, they argued, following Riker (1965), that citizens make rational choices about political participation. First, a person decides whether to participate. If the decision is yes, then the person makes a choice about the most comfortable or efficacious mode in which to channel this participation in the context of alternative participatory modes (Vedlitz and Veblen, 1980:45).

Shin and Everson (1980:11), studying three Illinois cities, offered similar conclusions: "Contacting is a nearly independent form of political activity." Their correlations of contacting with campaign, communal, and voting activities were somewhat higher than those found by Verba and Nie, but their Pearson coefficients ranged only from .10 to .25. Shin and Everson also speculated about the reasons for this apparent independence of contacting from other forms of participation. They argued that "the need for contacting may result from lack of experience or involvement in other, broader, forms of political participation" (Shin and Everson, 1980:32). Presumably there are reasons for this alleged lack of experience in other forms, although Shin and Everson avoided further speculation. They also implied that particularized contactors are "citizens whose participation is otherwise minimal," "irregular," and "largely limited to contacting" (Shin and Everson, 1980:6).

Only two studies could be found that argued for a model of contactors as political activists and for contacting as an integrated part of the political activist stratum. Eisinger (1972), in his Milwaukee study, found fairly substantial associations between contacting and other forms of political activity. The Pearson coefficients ranged primarily from .46 to .74 for white respondents and from .52 to .87 for black respondents in his survey. Eisinger (1972:62) concluded that "there is a substantial positive relationship between contacting public officials and participation in conventional electoral and party politics." His summary statement is strongly worded: "Contactors, then, comprise a significant portion of the city's politically active stratum. Contact is a part of the entire syndrome of political activity. As such it is possible to argue that the contact experience and participation in other forms of activity interact to influence, lead into, or reinforce one another. The public official is not dealing in most cases with an isolated individual when he responds to an individually generated contact" (1972:64).

Steger, Vertz, and Wirth (1982) used both intercorrelations and factor analysis to measure the distinctiveness of communalism and contacting. They used two questions about each from a national survey and found that all four items were fairly strongly related. They called this single cluster of participation "problem-solving behavior" and concluded that communalism and contacting are part of a single dimension of activity.

Collecting Evidence in Birmingham

Most previous research supports a model of particularized contacting as the act of an isolated, parochial participant involved in essentially nonpolitical behavior in pursuit of immediate, personal, narrowly defined self-interest. Contactors engage minimally, at best, in other modes of participation. Three sets of data were collected in Birmingham to test this proposition. The University of Alabama's Capstone Poll conducted two random-digit dialing telephone surveys of 550 and 556 adult residents in January 1983 and January 1984 in which the respondents were asked a variety of questions about their political participation. These two surveys were merged to create a sample size of 1,106. The third survey was based on a systematic random sample of 276 residents who had contacted the Mayor's Office of Citizens Assistance during January–April, 1984. The Capstone Poll also conducted this latter survey in early May 1984 and included an identical battery of participation questions.

The research strategy pursued with these data sets was to consider statistics from the combined mass surveys as indexing the average Birmingham resident and those from the MOCA contactors' survey as representing the average particularized contactor in Birmingham. The content of these contacts was investigated in MOCA records and was matched with respondents' own assessments of why they had contacted. There was virtually 100% agreement between the two sources. And all but one of the contacts (which was eliminated from the analysis) had apparently particularized rather than broad or social referents. Here "particularized" refers primarily to personal benefits (with some overlap with neighborhood benefits). Almost all of these contacts represented requests and complaints about problems located less than one block from the contactor's front door. Almost one-third of the contacts constituted complaints about overgrowth of vacant lots and ditches. Abandoned buildings, sewage and flooding problems, street and sidewalk repair, and problems with junk and abandoned cars accounted for approximately 10 percent each of the sample of contacts. Most of the rest concerned animal control, traffic conditions, malfunctioning street lights, and crime.

Four kinds of participation questions were asked of both samples: talking about politics, voting, communal political activity, and campaigning. Questions concerning talking about politics were taken from Matthews and Prothro (1966). They ask if the respondent ever talked "about public problems—that is, what's

happening in the country or in your community—with members of
your family, friends, co-workers, government officials or people in
politics, community leaders such as church or club leaders, or
members of another race." Voting questions asked respondents
whether they had voted in the 1980 presidential election and if they
had voted in all, most, some, or none of five types of elections since
they had been old enough to vote: presidential, general elections
for governor, primary elections for governor, local elections such
as for mayor or sheriff, and neighborhood association elections in
Birmingham's Citizen Participation Program.

Two communal political activity questions asked whether respondents had ever worked with others in their community to try to
solve some community problem and whether they had ever taken
part in forming a new group or a new organization to try to solve
some community problem. They were also asked whether they had
ever contacted a government official outside Birmingham about
some need or problem, whether they had held an office in a political
party or been elected or appointed to a government job, or whether
they had belonged to a political group such as a Democratic or
Republican club or other political organization. Questions about
campaign activities asked whether respondents had ever given
money or bought tickets or anything to help someone who is trying
to win an election, whether they had gone to any political meetings
in connection with an election, whether they had done any work to
help a candidate, and whether they had talked with people in an
effort to persuade them to vote for or against any candidates.

The basic proposition to be examined, following evidence produced by most of the research literature, is that contactors are
isolated parochials and that they will exhibit significantly lower
participation rates than the average citizen. I will test the proposition by comparing means and percentages of the mass and contactor samples and computing the significance of differences
between them.

Birmingham's Particularized Contactors

Table 4–1 contains percentages of the mass and contactor samples who talked about public problems with various others. The
results are mixed. Particularized contactors talk about public prob-

Table 4-1. **Talk about Public Problems**

Other parties in conversation	Citizenry (A)	Contactors (B)	Difference (A − B)
Family	83.8	85.2	*−1.4*
Friends	88.8	87.5	1.3
Co-workers	70.5	68.3	2.2
Public officials	38.4	56.9	*−18.5*[a]
Community leaders	60.1	73.0	*−12.9*[a]
Members of another race	68.3	67.8	.5

Note: Italics highlight evidence that contactors are more active than the average citizen.
[a]Significant at .001.

lems with public officials and community leaders at a substantially and significantly higher rate than citizens at large, contrary to the research hypothesis. Contactors talk more with members of their families but not at a significantly higher rate. Differences in the other categories are small and not significant but are in the hypothesized direction. Contactors talk politics "instrumentally," where it counts—that is, with officials and leaders. Data in table 4–1 certainly do not suggest that contactors are isolated parochials, at least not in comparison with the average citizen in Birmingham.

Table 4–2 presents data on the voting behavior of citizens and contactors. The evidence overwhelmingly indicates that contactors vote in all kinds of elections at significantly higher rates than the average citizen in Birmingham. In fact, the percentage point differentials in favor of the contactors range from 15.2 to 21.5 and are all statistically significant. Contactors are voting activists rather than isolated parochials as compared with the average citizen.

Table 4–3 includes evidence regarding communal political activity as well as supralocal contacting, officeholding, and membership in a political club. Once again, contactors are more active than the average citizen in all these examples of participation, and four out of five are significant and sizable. Contactors' communal participation is substantially greater than that for the citizenry at large and is significant at $p = .001$; contactors are much more

Table 4-2. **Voting Behavior**

Item	Citizenry (A)	Contactors (B)	Difference (A − B)
Voted in 1980 presidential election	72.4	87.6	−15.2a
Always voted in presidential elections	50.0	66.7	−16.7a
Always voted in gubernatorial elections	46.9	63.0	−16.1a
Always voted in gubernatorial primaries	39.0	54.2	−15.2a
Always voted in mayoral elections	36.6	58.1	−21.5a
Always voted in neighborhood elections	21.2	40.3	−19.1a

Note: Italics highlight evidence that contactors are more active than the average citizen.
aSignificant at .001.

active in their neighborhoods' efforts to solve public problems. They also contact state and federal officials more frequently, and more of them belong to political associations. Only one of the five tests of the research hypothesis is supported by the data in table 4–3.

Evidence on participation in campaign activities also indicates that contactors in Birmingham are not the isolated parochials that

Table 4-3. **Communal Political Activity**

Item	Citizenry (A)	Contactors (B)	Difference (A − B)
Worked with neighbors to solve community problems	51.9	67.5	−15.6a
Helped form a new group to solve neighborhood problems	19.4	31.4	−12.0a
Contacted a state or federal official	23.4	30.8	−7.4a
Held office	4.0	6.4	−2.4a
Belonged to a political association	12.1	17.8	−5.7a

Note: Italics highlight evidence that contactors are more active than the average citizen.
aSignificant at .05.

Table 4-4. Campaign Activities

Item	Citizenry (A)	Contactors (B)	Difference (A − B)
Gave money, bought tickets	41.5	50.5	− 9.0[a]
Attended campaign meetings	42.4	45.7	− 3.3[a]
Worked in campaign	31.7	48.5	−16.8[a]
Spoke for candidate	44.7	53.7	− 9.0[a]

Note: Italics highlight evidence that contactors are more active than the average citizen.
[a]Significant at .01.

Verba and Nie (1972) and others have claimed they are. Contactors are significantly more likely than the average citizen to give money to a candidate or party, to work for a candidate in a campaign, and to try to persuade others to vote for or against a candidate. Contactors' greater propensity to attend campaign meetings is not statistically significant. Once again, only one of the four tests of the research hypothesis is supported by the data in table 4–4. Contactors are campaign activists relative to the average citizen.

The proposition guiding this analysis postulated that contactors participate in other political activities at a significantly lower rate than the average citizen. Comparison of contactors with the average citizen seems fairer than comparison of contactors with voters where voting is concerned or with campaign activists where campaign activity is concerned. The data on Birmingham citizens and contactors permitted twenty-one separate tests of the proposition. None was confirmed. In fact, Birmingham contactors were found to be significantly more active in fifteen of the tests. Contactors are far above average in all modes of political participation, especially in voting and campaigning. The civic behavior of particularized contactors in Birmingham strongly suggests that they are complete political activists, not isolated parochials as the Verba and Nie model indicates.

Chapter 3 tested several of the conventional models designed to explain contacting and found that none of them successfully explained contact behavior in Birmingham. As a result, a new model was constructed. Chapter 4 tested the predominant model of the contactor as an isolated parochial and found it to be completely inappropriate as a description of the Birmingham contactor. As a result, a new model was offered. In the final chapter we reexamine the theory of contacting in an effort to explain why the previous models failed and to account for Birmingham's patterns of contacting and contactors.

5
Remodeling Contact Theory:

Who Contacts and Why?

The predominant theories of contacting are inadequate to explain patterns of citizen-initiated contact in Birmingham. None of the models of the relationship between SES and contacting found in the literature—positive, null, negative, and downward-opening parabola—could be found in Birmingham. Nor could a conception of the contactor as isolated parochial be found in Birmingham. This situation raises several troublesome questions. Are all the SES-contacting models suspect, or is Birmingham just unique? Can any *single* model explain contacting in all cities? Or are different models valid in different cities because cities are different? The answers to these and related questions lie in further examination of the theory and methodology of contact research. Theoretical problems that particularly need further exploration pertain to assumptions about the SES relationship with need for government services and civic attitudes. Methodological problems that require solution stem from differences between microanalysis and macroanalysis, between survey data from interviews with individuals and official archive data aggregated to the neighborhood level.

This final chapter reexamines a variety of theoretical and methodological issues in order to answer some of these troublesome questions and to evaluate the various models. To anticipate the conclusions reached in this final chapter, first, need seems paramount, and awareness or civic attitudes minor in importance. Second, neither microanalysis nor macroanalysis alone can definitively establish the model of contacting, but macroanalysis seems to produce more credible results. These arguments will be pursued later, after we have dealt with a theme introduced in the first chapter, the importance of who contacts and why.

The Importance of the SES-Contact Relationship

The relationship between SES and contacting is important primarily for two reasons. First, the socioeconomic causes or origins of contacting are partly responsible for determining the nature of the political system of a given municipality. This characteristic reflects the view that contacting is municipal political participation, and who participates in government is one of the defining qualities of any polity. Is contacting, as a form of political participation, dominated by one socioeconomic group, for example, wealthy, middle-class, or low-income citizens? Or do all three classes exhibit a roughly equal propensity to contact? A second reason for the importance of contacting is the distributional implication of an Adam Smith rule. If municipal bureaucratic agencies deliver services to eligible clients who request them but not to eligible clients who do not request them, response to demand is the operative decision rule governing service delivery (Coulter, 1983b). If demand is socioeconomically biased, then so is service distribution.

The relationship between citizens who initiate contacts and agencies who respond with service delivery links two of the basic elements of nonelectoral citizen participation in a democracy, that is, influence on government decisions and the consumption of public goods and services. Socioeconomic bias in the distribution of services is almost inevitable in an Adam Smith city if socioeconomic origins of contacting are biased. Table 5-1 presents some of the service distributional implications of alternative SES-contacting relationships.

Two assumptions support the logic of table 5-1. First, it is assumed, of course, that an Adam Smith rule governs service distribution. Second, it is assumed that both need and civic attitudes are necessary and exhaustive influences on contacting; some need and some appropriate civic attitudes are required to generate a contact. But the assumed relationships between SES and civic attitudes and between SES and need are left unspecified at this point. Civic attitudes, as a concept, incorporate political efficacy, interest, involvement, information, duty, and awareness.

Cincinnati (Thomas, 1982), Wichita (Sharp, 1982), Kitchener,

Table 5-1. Service Distributional Implications of Alternative SES-Contact Relationships in an "Adam Smith" Municipality

SES-contact relationship	Advantaged class(es)	Disadvantaged class(es)	Type of political system	Apparent major influence
Positive linear	wealthy	middle class and especially poor	oligarchy	civic attitudes
Downward-opening parabola	middle class	wealthy and poor	bourgeoisie	need combined with civic attitudes
Null	none	none	egalitarian	neither
Upward-opening parabola	wealthy and poor	middle class	polarized	need
Negative linear	poor	middle class and especially wealthy	proletarian	need

Canada (Brown, 1982), Garland (Vedlitz and Veblen, 1980), and other jurisdictions exhibit a positive relationship between measures of SES and contacting. Wealthy citizens initiate contacts at a higher rate than middle-class or poor citizens. The wealthy in these cities have a comparative advantage, and if the assumptions are correct, these cities have oligarchic political systems. Civic attitudes are clearly more important than need as an explanation of contact rate. In contrast, the middle class has a clear advantage over both wealthy and poor residents in Detroit (Bachelor, 1983; Jones et al., 1977), which has an essentially bourgeois political system. Need is assumed to be negatively related to SES, and awareness is assumed to be positively so and to interact multiplicatively to form the downward-opening parabola.

Houston (Mladenka, 1977) and Kansas City (Sharp, 1984b), for example, can be characterized as egalitarian political systems, since contact rates are virtually equal among all three SES classes. This pattern suggests that both need for services and civic attitudes are randomly distributed among the three groups. No SES group has a comparative advantage.

Analysis of Birmingham in chapter 3 suggests a polarized political system in which wealthy and poor residents contact local government at a disproportionately high rate. Middle-class residents have a comparative disadvantage. Finally, both Dallas and Houston (Vedlitz, Dyer, and Durand, 1980) manifest a negative relationship between SES and contacting, indicating that the poor have a comparative advantage over both middle-class and wealthy citizens. Need for service, in such a proletarian system, is the critical influence on contact behavior.

Unquestionably, the SES-contact relationship is important. In fact, it is one of the primary defining characteristics of an urban political system. It is in the context of this importance that theoretical and methodological issues are next discussed.

Theoretical Issues

Three sets of theoretical issues need rethinking. First, assumptions about relationships among SES, civic attitudes, need, and contacting must be questioned. Second, where both need and civic attitudes are important, their relative weights may vary among different political jurisdictions. Third, the definition and prominence of need should be established.

QUESTIONABLE ASSUMPTIONS

Proponents of two major schools of thought, the standard socioeconomic model and the need-awareness model, make several critical assumptions about variables that presumably intervene between socioeconomic status or well-being and contacting. Verba and Nie (1972), chief architects of the standard SES model, make three critical assumptions: (a) socioeconomic status has a positive, linear relationship with political efficacy, involvement, interest, duty, and information; (b) these five intervening civic attitudes bear a positive, linear association with propensity to contact; and (c) need for government service is irrelevant to contacting behavior. Certainly the assumption that need is irrelevant can be rejected. Several studies have shown, both logically and empirically, that contacting is an instrumental act and is related to need for government service.

The need-awareness model of Jones et al. (1977) makes the following assumptions: (a) both need and awareness are important to contacting; (b) need has a negative, linear relationship with SES; (c) awareness has a positive, linear relationship with SES. Jones et al. define awareness to include beliefs that government is responsible for satisfying citizens' needs, is capable of doing so and can be persuaded to act, and that the citizen has a channel of access to government through which to make a contact. Awareness and civic attitudes are similar.

It should be recalled that SES is simply a convenient surrogate for civic attitudes in one model and for need and awareness in the other. Unless SES actually bears the assumed relationships with intervening variables, and unless civic attitudes bear the assumed relationship with contacting, SES will not have the theoretically expected association with contacting. Therein lies the problem with both of the major contacting models; their theoretical assumptions are certainly questionable and possibly invalid.

Verba and Nie (1972:135) found a simple correlation coefficient of .45 between SES and civic orientations but only .10 between civic attitudes and contacting. Sharp (1982:112) found that most of the respondents in Wichita with low SES were characterized by high awareness and low-to-moderate need. Vedlitz and Veblen (1980:41) correlated education (an SES indicator) with interest in city government (a civic attitude) and found no significant association. Brown's (1982:224) findings indicate that the SES relationship with efficacy and interest is null but that the SES relationship with involvement and awareness is significant but small to moderate in size (gamma coefficients of .15 and .23, respectively). Need had nonsignificant relationships with both awareness and involvement. Similarly, interest, involvement, and awareness correlations with contacting were significant but only .18, .14, and .22, respectively, while efficacy's coefficient with contacting was nonsignificant.

Sharp (1984c:16) found that education and interest had nonsignificant relationships with perceived need, in a multiple regression equation based on Kansas City data. Income had a significant but tiny coefficient. Steger, Vertz, and Wirth (1982:26) reported nonsignificant relationships between perceived government responsiveness and contacting and between SES and perceived responsiveness. Dran and Smith (1984:17–18) discovered that SES was *positively* related to need in Detroit, for issue contacting. They also found no relationship between SES and awareness, and a nonsignificant association between efficacy and contacting. Friedman (1974:29, 35–38, 45–46) reported that the tau_c coefficient of association between efficacy and education, socioeconomic level, occupation, and income in Alberta, Canada, varied from .13 to .22—not very strong. The association between contacting and three socioeconomic variables in two Alberta samples and Great Britain was about the same. Efficacy's association with complaining was only .10. Attitude toward complaining (whether or not complaining is useful) had only weak relationships to actual complaining (.08, .10, and .14).

The relationship between efficacy and contacting is illustrative. In many cases efficacy has only a very weak or nonsignificant association with contacting. It appears that none of the standard indexes of efficacy applies well to citizens who perceive a reason for complaining about or for requesting a service. They may simul-

taneously believe (a) that government is unresponsive and uncaring
and (b) that citizens must adopt a more aggressive stance vis-à-vis
government because government is unresponsive and uncaring.
Contacting is not an ordinary mode of political participation. It is
the instrumental and dissonant element of participation (Mierwald
and Comer, 1986).

The assumed relationships were found to be nonexistent or nonsignificant in many studies of contacting. The numerous instances
in which the assumptions were untrue and the great variety of SES-
contacting relationships found in several American cities strongly
suggest that the substantive linkage between SES and contacting is
more complicated than most researchers have admitted. The assumptions are simply not dependable. When the positive model or
the parabolic model of Jones et al. works (or appears to work), it
may work (or may appear to work) for reasons other than the
theory stipulated in the relevant contact model.

APPROPRIATE WEIGHTING OF NEED AND AWARENESS

Some cities have neighborhood political organization in varying
degrees and some do not. Some cities have centralized complaint
management and some do not. The varying strength of these two
institutions probably seriously affects the relative influence of need
and awareness on contacting across American cities. The Jones et
al. mathematical model of need-awareness interaction weights both
components equally. In some cities, equal weighting might be satisfactory. But in a city mobilized by either a neighborhood political
organization or a centralized complaint unit or both, the assumption that need and awareness have equal importance is questionable.

Neighborhood political organization can affect the distribution
of both civic attitudes and perceived need (Rich, 1979 and 1980;
Yates, 1977:51). Neighborhood political leaders can, of course,
mobilize their fellow citizens by informing them of the existence of
a centralized complaint agency if one exists. They can also en-
hance awareness by informing citizens about procedures for contacting various municipal government officials to make service
requests and by reassuring them about the propriety of doing so.

Neighborhood leaders can also serve as a direct channel of communication between citizen and government by taking citizens' service complaints directly to the relevant officials.

Neighborhood organization's most prominent mobilization function, however, might be to heighten citizens' perceptions of need for government services (Lamb, 1976; O'Brien, 1975). Perceived need is defined here as the difference between perceived reality and normative expectation about reality, in other words, between neighborhood conditions as a citizen comprehends them and citizen expectations about what those conditions *should* be.

Neighborhood organization can alter citizens' perceived need by altering both their comprehension of and their expectations about reality. It sharpens their perceptions of neighborhood conditions, raises their expectations about the quality of those conditions, and tells them that government is both responsible for eradicating undesirable conditions and responsive to citizen requests for service to do so. It tells them that conditions in their neighborhoods are inadequate, that other neighborhoods have better conditions and services, and that they deserve better conditions and services (Brown and Coulter, 1983; Sharp, 1984c). The result is citizen dissatisfaction.

It can, in addition, stimulate political cognition, interest in local government, psychological involvement in local politics, and a sense of civic duty (Haeberle, 1986), all basic attitudes of the standard socioeconomic model (Verba and Nie, 1972:125–27).

Both Vedlitz, Dyer, and Durand (1980) and Sharp (1984a) argued that information about the existence of a central complaint center is more evenly distributed, geographically and socioeconomically, in a city with such a center than are other types of political information. In fact, Vedlitz, Dyer, and Durand reasoned that "a centralized contacting system . . . may reduce the effect of awareness to the point at which contacts are substantially a function only of the need for services" (1980:65). Sharp also found that contact with Kansas City's centralized complaint unit was twice as strongly correlated with SES as contact with other channels ($r = -.41$ and $-.22$, respectively). In line with that result, the correlation coefficient between awareness of the centralized complaint center and SES, she found, was only half as large as that between awareness of other avenues of contacting and SES ($r = .337$ and $.728$, respectively).

Neighborhood organization probably heightens sense of perceived need most in neighborhoods with greatest needs. Centralized contacting systems tend to equalize distribution of awareness across categories of socioeconomic status by reducing the cost of acquiring information, especially influencing the poor, for whom information costs are higher (Vedlitz, Dyer, and Durand, 1980).

Numerous weightings are possible that produce various types of linear and parabolic relationships between SES and contacting. Jones et al. (1977:151) used the following multiplicative equation to express the interactive effect of awareness and need on contacting: $P = C_1 IN$, where P = propensity to contact, C_1 is a constant, I = information, and N = need. Perhaps a more accurate mathematical expression of the model would exponentially weight one of the terms, perhaps awareness, as follows: $P = C_1 I^e N$, where e is a positive number.

Such an exponentially weighted interactive equation would more accurately assign relative weights to each term. In a city such as Detroit, discussed in Jones et al. (1980), if need is negatively related to SES and awareness positively so, the exponent would probably be approximately positive unity and would disappear. In a city such as Birmingham or Dallas (Vedlitz, Dyer, and Durand, 1980) with a centralized complaint bureau, the exponent would be between positive unity and zero, indicating diminished relative importance of awareness due to the complaint agency's at least partial equalization of awareness across SES levels. Neighborhood political organization could have a similar effect by equalizing awareness, heightening perceived need, or both.

Existence of a "threshold effect" could also complicate relationships of SES to contacting, as noted by Sharp (1984b:42–47). The original need-awareness model stipulated that sufficient levels of both components are necessary to induce contact behavior, and it is assumed that there will be moderate levels of both need and awareness in the middle range of SES. Sharp suggested that there might be no population subgroup with sufficient levels of both need and awareness to increase contact propensity significantly above the population norm. She assumed that the overall average scores for need and awareness were the threshold points and found, for Kansas City, that no education subgroup was substantially above average on both need and awareness. Such an empirical situation could have serious effects for the SES-contacting relationship, even when SES bears the relationships with need and awareness theoretically assumed by the model. However, if one of these assumptions is not met, the contaminating effects of thresholds on the need-awareness model could be even more serious.

SPECIAL ISSUES OF NEED

Assumptions that SES relationships with need and awareness are *variable* and are based on the extent of political mobilization, including the ideas of differential weighting of need and awareness and a threshold effect, help to resolve or at least clarify some special issues surrounding the concept of need. Seven such issues are evident: social versus particularized referents, clientelism, voluntary versus mandatory contacts, objective versus subjective needs, small versus severe needs, cost of need satisfaction, and interaction of need with awareness.

Anyone can experience a need with either referent, but the literature seems to suggest that citizens with low SES make a higher rate of particularized-referent contacts and citizens with higher SES make a relatively larger number of social-referent contacts (Zuckerman and West, 1985). Similarly, research indicates that aggregate data analysis nets a higher proportion of particularized contacts and that survey research nets a higher proportion of social-referent contacts. The point is that citizens at different levels of SES may experience different types of need and, consequently, may generate contacts with different referents.

Second, Thomas (1982) has argued essentially that all citizens have a roughly equal intensity of need for government service and that only the kind of services needed varies by level of SES. High-income as well as low-income citizens need services and make contacts, but they contact different agencies in pursuit of different kinds of service. Thomas calls this characteristic "clientelism," since different government agencies have different SES clienteles.

In Thomas's view, need is paramount and SES is secondary in importance. For a group of citizens with a similar need, those with higher SES are more likely to contact. But presumably those with similar SES will have significantly different levels of need for a given service. The clientelism conception of need contrasts with the "unidimensional-linear" conception, which defines need as undifferentiated with respect to service type and negatively related to SES and assumes that, as SES increases, citizens satisfy more of their needs in the private sector rather than through government services.

The third issue, whether attempting to satisfy needs is voluntary or mandatory, is closely related to the clientele/unidimensional distinction. For example, need for emergency service could be considered nonvoluntary. When a citizen's automobile is stolen, he/she calls the police. When a residence catches on fire, an occupant calls the fire department. When someone has a serious accident or a heart attack, emergency medical service is contacted. Virtually all people behave in the same way under these conditions, so that there is a basically null relationship between SES and contacting for nonvoluntary types of services. Only need is relevant here, but need for emergency services is probably unrelated to SES.

Contacting to satisfy most needs, however, is probably a voluntary act. Most problems that citizens encounter are not emergencies, and there is no compulsion to contact government to seek a solution. Rather, a citizen exercises discretion about whether and when to initiate a contact; SES may be more important in this instance.

A fourth important definitional distinction involves whether need is "objective" or "subjective," that is, defined by the investigator and attributed to citizens or psychologically perceived by citizens. Clearly, perceived need is crucial. If an individual does not perceive a need, he/she is unlikely to initiate a contact. Aggregate data studies unfortunately do not permit measurement of perceived need; survey research cannot include measures of objective need. Whether objective or perceived need is more important has been largely a methodological issue. Microanalysis uses measures of individuals' perceived need, and macroanalysis explains contact as a function of neighborhood need defined by census variables. Logic should overrule methodological considerations here to establish the position that a citizen who *perceives* no need to initiate a contact will initiate no contact. Similarly, objectively defined serious needs will prompt contacts only if they are *perceived* as such by someone. The relationship between objective and perceived needs, therefore, is critical in defining need and its relationship to contacting. Sharp (1984c) has shown that objectively defined and subjectively perceived need bear a significant but modest association in Kansas City.

The very slight correlation between objective and perceived need suggests that individual citizens are differentially sensitive to identical objective problems. Social psychological exchange theory (Coulter, 1983a; Helson, 1964; Secord and Beckman, 1974; and Thibaut and Kelley, 1959) provides an explanation of this phenomenon and helps to account for the effect of need on contacting. Individuals have a more or less precise comprehension of the environmental reality or conditions in which they live in their communities. They also have a normative expectancy about what those environmental conditions *should* be. Discrepancy between what they think reality should be and their comprehension of the actual reality defines their perceptions of need. If their expectations are met or exceeded, they will be satisfied and will perceive few or no needs. If they reason that perceived environmental conditions are inferior to their expectations, they will perceive a need. If they detect a pothole in their streets but expect smooth streets, they will perceive a need for improved street conditions.

A fifth issue of need is difference between small needs and severe needs. Steger, Vertz, and Wirth (1982) measured both types of need in a national survey by asking respondents whether they thought each of fourteen problems was severe, small, or not a problem in their communities. They summed the number of times a respondent considered a problem severe or small across the fourteen problems. They found that respondents' SES was positively correlated with perceived small problems and was negatively correlated with perceived severe problems. In other words, higher SES people perceived a variety of small problems, and lower SES people perceived severe problems, but both perceived needs. They concluded "that there may be different models of problem-solving participation for different levels of socioeconomic status. Factors of area need . . . may take on different meanings for individuals of high, medium, and low SES levels" (Steger, Vertz, and Wirth, 1982:23). Similarly, Sharp reported a tau$_b$ correlation between objective need and problem perception across Kansas City neighborhoods of only .292.

Sixth, needs probably differ with respect to the citizen's estimated cost of satisfying them. A citizen with a need is more likely to express it to local government when its satisfaction appears unlikely to result in financial obligation, such as increased property taxes or individual assessments for sewer or street improvements. If the anticipated governmental response to a perceived need is free to the individual, the need is more likely to be expressed as a contact. Sharp (1984c), for example, found that fixed-income elderly residents in one Kansas City neighborhood did not ask local government for the service they wanted most—sidewalks—because they feared increased costs.

Finally, the interactive nature of need and awareness might be more complicated than most researchers have assumed. Jones et al. (1980) argued that some need and some awareness are necessary to produce contact. If perceived need becomes severe enough, however, the unaware citizen will probably acquire the necessary awareness. If neighborhood problems become bad enough, a resident will eventually ask family, friends, and acquaintances whom to contact for help. Similarly, a citizen who perceives no serious problems but who becomes clearly aware of government's responsibility and responsiveness, might become less satisfied with neighborhood conditions and might begin to perceive at least small needs for government service. In other words, extreme need can generate awareness where there was none; extreme awareness can give birth to perception of problems and need for government services.

In fact, with careful examination the concept of awareness virtually dissolves into unimportance, if not basic irrelevance. It is probably unreasonable to assume that very many adults living in American cities are so profoundly ignorant that they (a) actually do not know that "city hall" or the mayor is responsible for public services and (b) actually do not know how to use a telephone. Very little real "awareness" is needed, and the tenuous relationship between civic attitudes such as efficacy and contacting has already been demonstrated.

Verba, in summarizing the empirical evidence from surveys of contact experience in a large variety of nation-states, including both developed and developing countries, conceptually defined the term "parochial awareness":

> A contrast exists between parochial awareness and expectation, on the one hand, and measures of broader political involvement. The latter measures are closely related to education and status as well as to exposure to the mass media. Parochial awareness, in contrast, does not depend on skills and resources associated with education or status. Individuals who may be uninvolved in broader political matters because of lack of education are as aware of the potential for government aid to themselves as their compatriots of higher socioeconomic levels. The former are, in fact, more likely to feel dependent on government. [1978:26]

Parochially aware citizens are those who think government could help solve some particularistic problem. Verba argued that such awareness is most frequent among persons who have experienced government services but are dissatisfied with them. Citizens appear to learn that government might be capable of helping them solve their particular problems if they have ever received some government services. The fact that the services were not satisfactory merely increases that awareness (Verba, 1978:25).

Need is primary and awareness is at most secondary in their interactional or conditional effects on contacting. Thomas has presented evidence that, because contacting is instrumental, it "should be primarily a function of what needs the individual perceives in the relevant service area" (Thomas, 1982:512–14). That notion is also consistent with Brown's conclusion "that the impact of need upon contacting is not strongly conditional on . . . level of awareness" (Brown, 1982:226) but "that the impact of awareness on contacting is largely conditional on the presence of some but not an excessive degree of need" (Brown, 1982:225). Sharp (1984a) found that, for respondents who perceived no need, contacting was strongly associated with SES. However, for citizens with substantial perceived needs, contacting and SES have only a negligible association. Clearly need and awareness do not always have a straightforward multiplicative impact on contacting.

Failure to consider these issues involved with need is probably an important reason why different studies of contacting have produced such a variety of conclusions about the SES-contacting relationship. Social and particularized contacts are mixed in the literature. Some studies treat the SES-contact relationship as unidimensional and linear; others assume it is multidimensional or clientelistic. Most surveys combine voluntary and mandatory service contacts; aggregate data studies usually do not. Most surveys define need as subjective perception of problems in the respondents' neighborhoods; aggregate data studies use census definitions of "objective" need in neighborhoods. Both fail to take into account citizens' expectations about what their neighborhoods should look like.

Most studies neglect consideration of severe and small needs, each of which may spur citizens of different SES levels to contact. Virtually no studies consider perceived contactor cost as a possible constraint on contacting. Citizens who perceive that satisfaction of their needs will cost money might be less likely to express them. Most studies do not give enough emphasis to the instrumental and dissonant character of contacting and therefore fail to convey the predominance of need in generating a contact. Failure to specify precise conceptual and operational definitions of need might well explain the differences between contradictory findings produced by contact studies.

Methodological Issues: Micro versus Macro

Many studies' findings appear to be at least partly if not substantially methodological artifacts. Survey research usually finds a positive linear relationship between SES and contacting, and aggregate data analysis usually finds some evidence of a negative relationship. That is, microanalysis confirms the importance of civic attitudes, and macroanalysis indicates the significance of

Table 5-2. **Relationship between Type of Methodology and SES-Contact Association**

	Methodology		
Association	Survey	Aggregate	Total
Positive	13	0	13
Null	4	1	5
Negative	0	7	7
Total	17	8	25

Note: df = 2.   Cramer's *V* = .80. χ^2 = 16.07.   *p* = .005.

need. Table 5-2 presents evidence to substantiate this conclusion. The data in this contingency table come from table 2-3. Findings from the current study of Birmingham have also been included.

Research findings have been filed in three mutually exclusive categories. The positive category contains all those studies that found a moderate-to-strong relationship between SES and contacting and therefore indicate civic attitudes as the cause of contacting. The null category contains results that indicate a negligible association or no association between SES and contact. The negative category contains those studies that found either a completely negative association or a parabolic relationship, both of which indicate a significant role for need in generating contacts.

Cross-tabulation of research results (positive, null, or negative) by research methodology (microanalysis or macroanalysis) strongly supports the assertion that results tend to be methodological artifacts. The chi-square value (16.07) in table 5-2 indicates that the bivariate distribution is statistically extremely significant. The Cramer's *V* measure of association between the two nominal scales is .80, revealing a strong relationship. It is assumed that the direction of causation is from methodology to result. Choosing a method is, to a substantial extent, choosing the result. Microanalysis emphasizes civic attitudes; macroanalysis emphasizes need.

Three studies of the same city using two different methods illustrate the micro-macro methodological dilemma. Dran and Smith's

(1984) microanalysis of Detroit found a positive, linear association, confirming the significance of civic attitudes. Macroanalysis of the same city in Jones et al. (1977) and Bachelor (1983) produced a downward-opening parabolic relationship, indicating that need is at least equally important. Could this discrepancy be attributed totally or partially to methodological differences? The tentative answer seems to be "yes." This is a difficult question whose final answer awaits analysis of a data set linking municipal archival contact records with survey research from the same city in the same period of time—in other words, surveying contactors from government agency archives and contextuating individuals from a random sample of adults.

Differences in data sets collected with micro- and macroanalytic methods are stark and important. The unit of analysis in survey research is the individual respondent. Microanalytic studies of contacting, as a result, overemphasize the importance of individual characteristics, especially psychological characteristics such as civic attitudes, and virtually exclude variables that describe the individual's social milieus. Microanalytic studies use no contextual variables to describe neighborhood socioeconomic or physico-environmental structure in which the individual lives. The latter is especially important with respect to the possible presence in the individual's neighborhood of negative externality fields that tend to generate complaints and service requests.

Survey data have several potentially serious validity problems. They probably include contacts that were *not* made because of respondents' faulty recall, lying, and misunderstanding of the question. They probably exclude contacts that *were* made because of respondents' faulty recall. Chapter 2 documented some of the problems that result from the time constraint placed on a contact question in a survey, that is, cases in which the respondent was asked whether he/she had contacted a local government official during the last year, last two years, or ever.

Similarly, a survey that simply asks one straightforward contact question is likely to elicit responses that differ from those produced by one that asks the question for each of a long list of specific municipal officials or agencies. Evidence from the two Birmingham mass surveys described earlier supports this argument

(Coulter, 1985). The estimated contact rates for Birmingham adults in the two surveys are 31.6 percent and 29 percent when respondents were asked the general question "Have you ever contacted a local government official about a problem or to request a service?" The contact rate estimate is significantly different, however, when respondents are asked the specific question "have you ever contacted the Street and Sanitation Department (or another specific department) about a problem or to request a service?" For example, 32.4 percent of the respondents who said "no" to the earlier general question said "yes" to a later specific question about contacting the Street and Sanitation Department. Even larger percentages of those who claimed no contact in response to the general question admitted that they had contacted the police and fire departments. Smaller percentages of "general question" noncontactors later admitted contacting each of seven other municipal departments. This evidence strongly suggests the unreliability of microanalytic results based on the single general question about contacting, as found in most studies. If survey estimates of the rate of contacting can vary that much, depending on whether one general question is asked or several specific ones, then estimates of who contacts and why are equally suspect, especially for studies using only the general-contact question.

Also, most surveys failed to ask respondents *how many* contacts they had initiated, thus assuming that contacting is measured as either none or one for each respondent. Undoubtedly, many respondents have contacted more than once. Survey data also include both social- and particularized-referent contacts, and differentiating between them is probably considerably harder than previous researchers have suspected. Similarly, both mandatory contacts (e.g., emergency calls to police and fire departments) and voluntary contacts are usually included without differentiation.

Statistical analysis that can, technically speaking, be legitimately performed on survey data is somewhat limited. Cross-tabulation and contingency analysis (using various measures of association) are sometimes the only modes of statistical analysis available. It is therefore impossible to measure the association between two variables while controlling the effect of more than one other variable unless a very large (and expensive) sample is available. Only a very large sample will yield enough contactors for analysis. Some statisticians argue that regression analysis is technically invalid with survey data and can produce untrustworthy results (Freeman, 1965). Macroanalytic studies use spatially defined social aggregates as the basic unit of analysis, for example, census tracts, politically defined neighborhoods, or school districts. It can be argued that contacts are initiated not by aggregate units but only by individuals. Aggregate data on contacts come from government records and are incomplete for several reasons. Regardless of which agency's records are used, agency officials probably do not record *all* contacts. For example, they probably do not record telephone requests for information that can be given easily and immediately on the phone or for ridiculous complaints. And if an agency were to record *all* contacts, its data would still include only contacts with that agency for a given time period, not all contacts in the municipality. This is a problem for even a centralized complaint agency, since citizens invariably continue to initiate many calls to each of a host of other city agencies. If a single agency's archives are used, the relationship found between SES and contact might be unique to that agency. Contact data from a central complaint agency, a business license office, and a street and sanitation department might produce rather different relationships between SES and contacting.

Since social aggregates are the unit of analysis in macroanalysis, investigators overemphasize social explanation and completely neglect individual contactors' characteristics. Furthermore, macroanalysis assumes that each contactor is roughly at his/her neighborhood's mean for income, education, housing value, or whatever SES variable is used. Similarly, aggregate data analysis assumes that each contactor perfectly translates his/her neighborhood's objective need into perceived need and a contact. It is possible, of course, that both assumptions are literally or statistically true (i.e., the average contactor does closely resemble the average resident of his/her neighborhood). But it is equally or perhaps more plausible that neighborhood complainers are atypical in their neighborhoods, for example, whites in majority black or Hispanic neighborhoods, upper-income residents of middle-income neighborhoods, middle-income residents in lower-income neighborhoods, owners of more expensive homes in less attractive neighborhoods, and so forth. Contacting might be generated by perceived socioeconomic or racial differences between the contactor and the social aggregate in which he/she lives. In this case, contactors are sensitive to neighborhood negative externalities that the average resident fails to detect, perhaps because they have higher expectations than the average resident or different expectations.

Aggregate data analysis fails both to measure need and awareness directly and to test the linkage between either of these and their presumed hypothetical antecedent (SES) and effect (contacts). And macroanalysis measures objective need, not the more important perceived need. Finally, macroanalysis probably examines particularized contacts almost to the exclusion of broad-referent contacts. Broad-referent needs are probably expressed predominantly in government public hearings and to elected officials and candidates during campaigns and are simply not recorded in government records.

If a researcher attributes neighborhood behavior to individuals, he/she risks committing the ecological fallacy. On the other hand, if he/she attributes individual behavior to neighborhoods, he/she risks committing the individualistic fallacy. Both of these fallacious attributions disregard the canons of logic and statistics. This methodological difficulty might be alleviated if contactors listed in government agency records were surveyed and respondents in a large sample were aggregated to the neighborhood level. This research strategy would combine individual and aggregate analysis and would provide insight into the extent to which findings generated by one method alone are artifacts of that method. It does seem fair to conclude, however, even without using the ideal research strategy, that surveys tend to confirm the standard SES model and that aggregate data analyses tend to emphasize the importance of need in explaining contacting.

Final Thoughts on Birmingham Contacting

Two of the most important facts about political participation in Birmingham might be that the city operates the Mayor's Office of Citizens Assistance and has an active, well-organized neighborhood movement. The city is organized into ninety-three neighborhoods, each of which elects its own officers every two years and annually receives funding from federal and local sources. The ninety-three neighborhood presidents elect delegates to twenty-two multineighborhood communities, which in turn select representatives who by law meet periodically with the mayor and council. Neighborhood leaders have directed a considerable amount of political energy toward improving municipal services. The joint effect of MOCA and the neighborhood movement has been to make Birmingham a politically mobilized city at the grass roots. Political mobilization reallocates need and awareness across spatial and socioeconomic groups, for example, by making less aware citizens more aware and by intensifying perception of need among the more needy.

Political mobilization engendered by MOCA and neighborhood organization has presumably made Birmingham's lower-income residents more aware of government's responsibility for service and responsiveness to citizen initiatives, and more perceptive of their problems and needs. Upper-income residents, at the same time, are also highly aware of government's responsibility and responsiveness and perceive considerable need for government services to protect their neighborhood property values. Middle-income residents have become *relatively* less aware and less perceptive than the newly sensitized lower-income citizens. This sequence of events seems to characterize Birmingham's situation (Haeberle, 1986).

Risks of inequitable service distribution in a polarized city such as Birmingham, with an upward-opening parabolic relationship between SES and contacting and an Adam Smith rule, are serious. The middle class may be relatively underserved. Such an inequitable distribution could produce a political backlash against city government for favoring the rich and poor compared with the middle class. If the middle class is large enough, the backlash could have serious implications. If it is small, it might remain a minority that continues to suffer from service discrimination. On the other hand, the Adam Smith rule in a city with a U-shaped relationship between SES and contacting may be defended as simply supplying service where it is most needed.

Conclusions

This book begins and ends with the same theme: citizen-initiated contacting of government officials is important and differs from other, more conventional types of political behavior, such as voting. Research on contacting has produced several conflicting models of the relationship between SES and contacting and two diametrically opposite models of the contactor as citizen. Contacting in Birmingham does not conform to any of the SES-contacting models; fitting a curve to the Birmingham data produces a different model, one emphasizing two kinds of need, with explanatory power as great or greater than almost all other contact models in the literature. Nor does the Birmingham contactor resemble the predominant model of contactor as parochial. Rather, Birmingham's contactors regularly engage in a diverse set of political activities.

Confusion and disagreement characterize the literature primarily because of theoretical and methodological problems. Theoretical assumptions about the linkage between SES and contacting prove not to be valid. They are of two sorts: (a) higher SES leads to higher levels of certain civic attitudes that in turn impel individuals to engage in all kinds of political participation, including contacting; and (b) the positive SES-awareness correlation and negative SES-need correlation produce a need-awareness interactional model in which middle-class residents contact most. The standard SES model and the need-awareness model make interesting theory, but the findings of most contact studies provide either contradictory evidence or little support. Similarly, the null model is unsatisfactory. Contacting is an important pattern of political behavior and can be explained at least partially. In contrast, a need model is theoretically most appealing. Citizens contact government because they need services. They need services because their neighborhoods fail to meet their expectations, and they desire to improve or protect their neighborhood environment.

Methodological problems center on differences between micro- and macroanalysis. Microanalysis, based on survey research, generally finds SES to be important, even when it is probably not and even though the requisite theoretical assumptions about SES-contact linkage are inaccurate. The basic dependent variable, contacting, usually defined by one basic survey question, appears to be highly unreliable and invalid. Macroanalysis, based on archival data, generally finds need to be important, and the conclusion of this book is that it is.

Activities intended to choose government personnel and activities intended to influence the choices of government personnel *are* different. The former is probably dominated by civic attitudes, indicates basic support for the political system, and represents the traditional role of the citizen. In contrast, contacting is dominated by need for government services, motivated by specific dissonance with the political system's current level of performance, and represents the role of the citizen as consumer in a service polity. Contacting is consumer politics.

References

Almond, Gabriel, and Sidney Verba. 1965. *The Civic Culture*. Princeton: Princeton University Press.

Altes, J. A., and R. E. Mendelson. 1980. "East St. Louis." In D. M. Johnson and R. M. Veach, eds., *The Middle-Sized Cities of Illinois*, pp. 89–121. Springfield, Ill.: Sangamon State University.

Bachelor, Lynn W. 1983. "Service Equity and Citizen Complaints: A Study of the Resolution of Service Delivery Complaints by the Detroit Ombudsman Office." Paper presented at the annual meeting of the American Political Science Association, Chicago, September 1–4.

Banfield, Edward C., and James Q. Wilson. 1983. *City Politics*. New York: Vintage.

Brody, Richard, and Paul Sniderman. 1977. "From Life Space to Polling Place: The Relevance of Personal Concerns for Voting Behavior." *British Journal of Political Science* 7 (July):142–77.

Brown, Karin, and Philip B. Coulter. 1983. "Subjective and Objective Measures of Police Service Delivery." *Public Administration Review* 43 (January–February):50–58.

Brown, S. D. 1982. "The Explanation of Particularized Contacting: A Comparison of Models." *Urban Affairs Quarterly* 18 (December): 217–34.

Burnett, A., K. Cole, and G. Moon. 1983. "Political Participation and Resource Allocation." In M. A. Busteed, ed., *Developments in Political Geography*, pp. 307–35. London: Academic Press.

Campbell, Angus, Philip E. Converse, Warren Miller, and Donald Stokes. 1960. *The American Voter*. New York: John Wiley.

Coulter, Philip B. 1983a. "Close Encounters of the Bureaucratic Kind: The Social Psychology of Police-Citizen Interaction." Paper presented at the annual meeting of the American Political Science Association, Chicago, September 2.

Coulter, Philip B. 1983b. "Inferring the Distributional Effects of Bureaucratic Decision Rules." *Policy Studies Journal* 12 (December):347–56.

Coulter, Philip B. 1985. "Citizen-Initiated Contacting: A Methodological Exploration of Rates and Reasons." Paper presented at the annual meeting of the American Political Science Association, New Orleans, September 2.

Cox, Kevin R. 1982. "Housing Tenure and Neighborhood Activism." *Urban Affairs Quarterly* 18 (September):107–29.

Dran, Ellen M., and Russell L. Smith. 1984. "Citizen-Initiated Contacting: One More Look." Paper presented at the annual meeting of the Midwest Political Science Association, Chicago, April 12.

Eisinger, Peter K. 1972. "The Pattern of Citizen Contacts with Urban Officials." In Harlan Hahn, ed., *People and Politics in Urban Society*, pp. 43–69. Beverly Hills, Calif.: Sage.

Elazar, Daniel. 1984. *American Federalism: A View from the States*. New York: Harper and Row.

Freeman, Linton C. 1965. *Elementary Applied Statistics*. New York: John Wiley.

Friedman, Karl A. 1974. *Complaining: Comparative Aspects of Complaint Behavior and Attitudes toward Complaining in Canada and Britain*. Beverly Hills, Calif.: Sage.

Haeberle, Steven H. 1986. "Good Neighbors and Good Neighborhoods: Comparing Demographic and Environmental Influences on Neighborhood Activism." *State and Local Government Review* 18 (Fall):109–16.

Helson, Harry. 1964. *Adaptation-Level Theory*. New York: Harper.

Hero, Rodney. 1986. "Explaining Citizen-Initiated Contacting of Government Officials: SES, Perceived Need, or Something Else?" *Social Science Quarterly* 67 (September):626–35.

Hirschman, Albert. 1970. *Exit, Voice, and Loyalty*. Cambridge, Mass.: Harvard University Press.

Jacob, Herbert. 1972. "Contact with Governmental Agencies: A Preliminary Analysis of the Distribution of Government Services." *Midwest Journal of Political Science* 16 (February):123–46.

Jones, Bryan D., S. R. Greenberg, C. K. Kaufman, and J. Drew. 1977. "Bureaucratic Response to Citizen Initiated Contacts: Environmental Enforcement in Detroit." *American Political Science Review* 71 (March):148–65.

Jones, Bryan D., S. R. Greenberg, and J. Drew. 1980. *Service Delivery in the City*. New York: Longman.

Lamb, Curt. 1976. *Political Power in Poor Neighborhoods*. New York: Schenkman.

Lehnen, R. G. 1976. *American Institutions, Political Opinion, and Public Policy*. Hinsdale, Ill.: Dryden Press.

Levy, Frank, Arnold Meltsner, and Aaron Wildavsky. 1974. *Urban Outcomes*. Berkeley: University of California Press.

Lipsky, Michael. 1980. *Street-Level Bureaucracy*. New York: Russell Sage.

Matthews, Donald C., and James Prothro. 1966. *Negroes and the New Southern Politics*. New York: Harcourt, Brace and World.

Mierwald, Robert D., and John C. Comer. 1986. "Complaining as Participation." *Administration and Society* 17 (February):481–500.

Milbrath, Lester W., and M. L. Goel. 1977. *Political Participation*. Skokie, Ill.: Rand McNally.

Mladenka, Kenneth R. 1977. "Citizen Demand and Bureaucratic Response: Direct Dialing Democracy in a Major American City." *Urban Affairs Quarterly* 12 (March):273–90.

O'Brien, David J. 1975. *Neighborhood Organization and Interest Group Processes*. Princeton: Princeton University Press.

Rich, Richard C. 1979. "The Roles of Neighborhood Organizations in Urban Service Delivery." *Urban Affairs Papers* 1 (Fall):81–93.

Rich, Richard C. 1980. "The Dynamics of Leadership in Neighborhood Organizations." *Social Science Quarterly* 60 (March):570–87.

Riker, William. 1965. *Democracy in the United States*. New York: Macmillan.

Secord, Paul, and Carl W. Beckman. 1974. *Social Psychology*. New York: McGraw-Hill.

Sharp, Elaine B. 1980. "Citizen Perceptions of Channels for Urban Service Advocacy." *Public Opinion Quarterly* (Fall):362–76.

Sharp, Elaine B. 1982. "Citizen-Initiated Contacting of Government Officials and Socioeconomic Status: Determining the Relationship and Accounting for It." *American Political Science Review* 76 (March): 109–15.

Sharp, Elaine B. 1984a. *A Multi-method Test of an Explanatory Model of Citizen-Initiated Contacting*. Final Report for National Science Foundation Project SES-8200435. Lawrence, Kans.: University of Kansas, Center for Public Affairs.

Sharp, Elaine B. 1984b. "Citizen Demand-Making in the Urban Context." *American Journal of Political Science* 28 (November):654–71.

Sharp, Elaine B. 1984c. "The Roots of Urban Demand Making." Paper presented at the 1984 annual meeting of the Midwest Political Science Association, Chicago, April 11–15.

Shin, Doh C., and David H. Everson. 1980. "Participation in the Verba-Nie Modes in Three Middle-Sized Cities." Paper presented at the annual meeting of the Midwest Political Science Association, Chicago, April 23–26.

Steger, Mary Ann, Laura L. Vertz, and Clifford J. Wirth. 1982. "Citizen-Initiated Contacts and Cooperative Activity on the Neighborhood Level." Paper presented at the annual meeting of the American Political Science Association, Denver, Colo., September 2–5.

Thibaut, John W., and Harold H. Kelley. 1959. *The Social Psychology of Groups*. New York: Wiley.

Thomas, John C. 1982. "Citizen-Initiated Contacts with Government Agencies: A Test of Three Theories." *American Journal of Political Science* 26 (August):504–22.

Thomas, John C. 1985. "Rethinking 'Groupless' Urban Politics: A Theory of Neighborhood Mobilization." Paper presented at the annual meeting of the American Political Science Association, New Orleans, August 28–September 1.

Vedlitz, Arnold, and Eric P. Veblen. 1980. "Voting and Contacting: Two Forms of Political Participation in a Suburban Community." *Urban Affairs Quarterly* 16 (September):31–48.

Vedlitz, Arnold, James A. Dyer, and Roger Durand. 1980. "Citizen Contacts with Local Governments: A Comparative View." *American Journal of Political Science* 24 (February):50–67.

Verba, Sidney. 1978. "The Parochial and the Polity." In Sidney Verba and Lucian Pye, eds., *The Citizen and Politics*, pp. 3–29. Stamford, Conn.: Greylock.

Verba, Sidney, and Norman H. Nie. 1972. *Participation in America: Political Democracy and Social Equality*. New York: Harper and Row.

Yates, Douglas. 1977. *The Ungovernable City*. Cambridge, Mass.: MIT Press.

Zuckerman, Alan S., and Darrell M. West. 1985. "The Political Bases of Citizen Contacting: A Crossnational Analysis." *American Political Science Review* 79 (March):117–31.

Index

Objective need. *See* Need
O'Brien, David J.: on neighborhood
   political mobilization, 79
Oligarchic political system: defined,
   73–75
Owner-occupied housing value, 21, 52.
   See also Property values

Parabolic model: *See* Need-awareness
   model
Parochial participation, 63–65, 85. *See
   also* Contacting, Political participation
Particularized contacting, 6–7, 19, 21–
   22, 24, 34, 37, 39–40, 81, 89, 91; defined, 4–5; rate, 15; as parochial, 63–
   65, 85; as activist, 65, 67–71; in Birmingham, 67–71
Party politics, 7, 65
Peoria, Ill., 23, 32; contact rate, 13
Perceived need: *See* Need
Polarized political system: defined, 73–
   75
Political activism, 65; in Birmingham,
   67–71
Political cognition, 26–27, 79; defined,
   18
Political efficacy, 22, 23, 24, 26–27, 30,
   31, 73, 77–78; defined, 18
Political interest, 22, 23, 73, 79; defined, 18
Political mobilization, 38, 78, 92. *See
   also* Neighborhood political leaders,
   Neighborhood political organization
Political participation: defined, 1; parochial, 5, 63–65, 85; societal, 5; and
   voting, 6–7; consumption of services
   as, 6, 22, 73, 94; and civic attitudes,
   18–19; problem-solving participation, 24, 65; cooperative activity, 24,
   64; in Birmingham, 26–56, 67–72;
   campaigning, 64–65, 67–70. *See also*
   Contacting, Particularized contacting, Instrumental activity
Political subcultures, 36

Portsmouth, England, 25, 33
Positive linear model. *See* Standard
   SES model
Problem-solving participation, 24, 65
Proletarian political system: defined,
   73–75
Property values: owner-occupied
   housing values, 21, 52–56; renter-
   occupied housing values, 25.
Prothro, James, 66
Psychological involvement in politics,
   73, 79; defined, 18

Quadratic equation, to test influences
   on contacting, 47–48
Quality of life, 2, 15, 17; in Birmingham, 40. *See also* Negative externalities

Race, 19, 22–23, 26, 31, 34–35, 46–47,
   90; in Birmingham, 46–56 passim.
   See also Chicanos
Renter-occupied housing value, 25.
   See also Property values
Representation, 2, 6
Responsiveness, 2; citizen sense of
   government, 18, 26–27, 35, 38, 77
Rich, Richard C.: on neighborhood or-
   ganization, 38, 78
Riker, William, 65
Rochester, N.Y., 31

St. Louis, Mo., 31
Secord, Paul: on need, 83
Self-reliance orientation, 22. *See also*
   Entitlement orientation
Service distribution, 3, 92; seasonal,
   41–43; spatial, 43–46. *See also* Distributional equity
Sharp, Elaine B., 5, 12, 13, 15, 26, 33,
   38, 73, 75; on null model, 21; on
   civic attitudes, 21, 24, 77; on failure
   of standard socioeconomic model,
   21–22; on entitlement orientation,

About the Author

Philip B. Coulter is Dean, College of Liberal Arts, University of New Orleans. Formerly he was director of the Institute for Social Science Research and professor of political science at The University of Alabama. He received a doctorate in political science from Rockefeller College of Public Affairs and Policy at the State University of New York at Albany. He teaches and does research in the areas of public policy analysis, research methods, and urban politics.

About the Institute

The University of Alabama established the Institute for Social Science Research in 1984 to promote and conduct social science research. The Institute seeks to advance the theory and methodology of social science disciplines and to respond to society's needs by applying social science to the study of social problems. ISSR is composed of three units: the Center for Social and Policy Analysis, the Capstone Poll, and the Research and Consulting Laboratory. Correspondence should be addressed to:

Institute for Social Science Research
319 ten Hoor Hall
The University of Alabama
Box 870216
Tuscaloosa, Alabama 35487–0216

About the Social Science Monograph Series

The Institute for Social Science Research and The University of Alabama Press publish the Social Science Monograph Series through a cooperative agreement. The Series includes analyses of social problems and theoretical or methodological works that significantly advance social science research in the judgment of Institute social scientists and of two or more anonymous referees. Conclusions expressed in the monographs are those of the authors and do not necessarily reflect the views of ISSR, The University of Alabama, or organizations that provide funds to support Institute research.